# Crank It Out!

## The Surefire Way to Become a Super-Productive Writer

**C. S. Lakin**

Crank it Out! The Surefire Way to Become a Super-Productive Writer

ISBN: 978-0-9861347-3-9

Cover by Humblenations.com

Ubiquitous Press

Morgan Hill, California

# Praise for *Crank It Out!*

"If you want to be a peak performer as a writer, *Crank It Out* is the book for you. Whether your habits just need a little tweaking or you are a chronic procrastinator, you will find many gems to empower you to be a consistent and productive writer.

Don't expect the usual productivity tools you've seen elsewhere—and certainly not at a surface level. Instead, Lakin takes a deep dive to help writer-readers assess what habits will work best for their particular personality and needs. Lakin has readers explore how all activities affect their productivity and energy level—from sugar and caffeine intake to sleep, exercise, and more. As a book development and publishing coach, I am recommending *Crank It Out* to writers I work with and highly recommend it to you!"

—Lisa Tener, author and creator of the Stevie Award-winning
Bring Your Book to Life® Program

"*Crank It Out!* is a practical hands-on guide for writers and other creatives who want to ramp up their output. Lakin's thoughtful analysis of the conditions that support (or inhibit) creative work shows you how to uncover your problem spots and offers specific fixes for each one. Most important, she'll teach you how prolific writers think.

Once you understand her ABCs of productivity—Attitude, Biology, Choices—you've got the tools you need to tweak your own creative process for more ideas, more words, more flow.

What to do when you're having a low-energy day, how to train your brain to focus, how to thwart self-sabotage and take control of the biological factors that make writing easier or harder—it's all there. This book is a must-read if you want to get more writing done in the time you have."

—Lynn Johnston, author of *The 30 Day Novel Workbook* and
*The 30 Day Romance Novel Workbook*

# Other Nonfiction Books by C. S. Lakin
## The Writer's Toolbox Series

## Other Books

# Contents

# Introduction

Productivity is often considered evidence of success. A person who is productive appears organized, proficient in his craft or skill. Employees and professors are expected to produce reports and papers to bring validation to their position.

As writers, we're concerned about being productive. Or, at least we should be.

Why? Well, how can we truly call ourselves writers if we aren't producing anything others can read? We can journal for years or toy with ideas. We might even pen a novel or two.

But at what point are we really "productive writers"?

In the professional sense—the career sense—we're not writers until we've published something.

I'd spent more than twenty years writing novels, acquiring literary agents, and submitting my work to publishers. Though I considered myself a writer—because the bulk of my time was dedicated to pursuing a writing career—I wasn't yet a *professional* writer. Not until my books became available to readers.

If you are aspiring to become a "true" writer and publish your books, at some point you have to think about productivity.

Why? Because once you connect with readers and start building a platform and fan base, you don't want to lose them. You may be content with writing and publishing just one book in your life. And that's fine. That's what Harper Lee did (up until the end of her life, when she published her second and last novel). But one book a lifetime is hardly the definition of a productive writer.

## Readers Expect a Steady Flow of Books

Writers who want to make a career out of writing books have to think about productivity. Readers discover a writer they like, and when they do, they'll usually read everything the author has written to date. That's what I do when I find an author whose writing I love. And that's exciting for an author; those are the kind of fans she wants.

But what happens if readers are waiting for the next book to come out . . . and it doesn't? While some fans will buy a favorite author's newest novel whenever it releases, there's a matter of traction to consider.

Simply said: readers want a steady flow of books from their favorite authors.

And how can an author truly gain traction (grow his fan base and sales) if he doesn't regularly put out books?

I've heard it said by many in the industry, best-selling authors included, that to really be a success (as far as productivity and sales go), a writer needs to release a book every three to four months.

While that's not likely to occur if you're solely on a traditional publishing track (since you are at the mercy of your publisher's schedule), it is something not only doable but desirable if you're self-publishing.

This isn't a hard-and-fast rule, but the logic is sound. Especially if you're trying to brand yourself.

You may be writing a series or two (or five). Your readers, now that you've hooked them with that first novel, are eagerly anticipating book number two. If you wait a year or more to release the next one in the series, and then wait another two years for the subsequent book, that momentum of growing readers may dwindle or fizzle out altogether.

And another consideration: How can you start making a steady (much less terrific) living from your books if you aren't cranking them out on a regular basis?

## What Cranking Is Not

Maybe the term "cranking it out" has negative connotations to you. I get that. We don't want to pump out garbage in the form of books just to meet our self-imposed deadline of "a book every three months." That will bring fresh meaning to the word *deadline*. Our careers will be dead in the water if all we focus on is the productivity and not the quality.

So the challenge for writers is to figure out how to be super productive and not compromise quality or integrity.

I believe writers can learn to "crank it out" in a good way. And while doing so may be easier for some and harder for others, I believe any writer can become super productive, and I'm going to show you how—with a threefold approach.

It's not just a matter of attitude, although that plays one part. I believe we need to consider way more than attitude to become super productive.

We're going to take a look at three key factors to productivity—and I think you're going to learn some new, fresh ideas on the subject. You might think of them as the "Productivity ABCs": attitude, biology, and choices.

Most importantly, we're going to tackle those obstacles to productivity—within and without.

## You Gotta Want It

Bottom line, though: before you can be a super-productive writer, you have to *want* to be. I'm guessing you do, because you're reading this material. And that's great.

Some authors write every day; they feel they have to. And maybe finding time to do so isn't an issue. Others write sporadically, sometimes putting writing off for months, for whatever reasons. But how frequently you sit down to write, or how many words you write a day, doesn't necessarily correlate to how much you produce.

Plenty of authors who hardly have an hour to write a week put out more books a year than some authors who write all day every day. And while being a "fast" writer may imply you can crank out more books than a "slow" one, that's also not necessarily the case (I put those words in quotes because *fast* and *slow* are a matter of perspective.) Do you recall the fable of the tortoise and the hare? Who won the race?

So, time does not equal productivity.

The trick is to get the most "productive" bang from each minute you write or engage in any writing-related activity.

You may have a picture in your mind of what success looks like to you—and that picture includes having numerous published books that sell well. You may have already written a book or a dozen books, but perhaps you're not feeling productive. You may argue that too many things are vying for your time, and you can't get into a schedule and mind-set to produce on a regular basis.

This is the challenge for just about every writer, and it's nothing new. Creatives of all types, throughout the centuries all across the globe, have had to figure out a way to carve out the time for their creative pursuits. Much of the time, creative people have to work other jobs to support themselves. Not all writers have the luxury of devoting huge chunks of time to their writing.

Like many of us, Nobel Prize–winning author Toni Morrison worked a full-time 9-5 job, with kids to raise, so she never had regular writing time. She'd write during breaks at work, hurriedly, or throughout the weekends or in the hours before dawn.

Surely you've heard of many writers who've "cranked out" books while working full-time. Or raising and homeschooling a passel of kids. I know one writer who'd penned six award-winning novels in that many years, wrote and published about six hundred magazine articles a year, while raising and homeschooling six kids under the age of ten (at that time). Not sure why six was a constant here, but it was.

Was I astonished? You bet. Envious? Oh yeah. I, who many consider crazy productive, felt like a worm when I learned about this author. How the heck did she manage all that? She must be a genius (well, she is, with multiple advanced college degrees in subjects that would blow your mind).

Okay, I chalked it up to her being an exception. An unusually organized person. Brilliant. Maybe borderline (or beyond?) neurotic. A type-AAA personality that would make my type A look like a wet noodle. No one can be productive like that. Or practically no one.

Or so I thought.

## Super-Productive Writers Are Just Crazy, Right?

I've gotten to know a number of super-productive authors. They each have published more than one hundred books, many of them best sellers. Many of them long, deep books—not eight-page picture books for children.

These authors also find time to teach, raise kids, conduct workshops, tour, go fishing or play golf, keep up a blog, teach online courses . . . and the list goes on.

What I learned about these authors that surprised me is this: they're not neurotic. They're not obsessed, foregoing sleep, burning the candle at both ends until they melt into a puddle of wax. They're actually quite balanced and level-headed. They show no hint of madness—as far as I can tell (other than the usual creative madness).

So, what's their secret?

I'm going to share some identifiers of productive writers with you. But keep this in mind: everyone is different, and what works for one writer may not work for you.

I often write and publish four or five full-length books a year, in addition to writing more than 100,000 words on my blog, guest posting, teaching workshops, and editing nearly full-time. I've found a way to live a balanced full life, making the most of my time and being super productive without going crazy.

I wasn't always that way. In fact, I was the ultimate slacker for many years. So I know the pitfalls, the excuses, and the struggles—as well as the hacks and perfect solutions to blasting any and all obstacles out of my way.

My aim in tackling this topic is to give you as much helpful insight into productivity as possible so you can become the highly productive writer you dream of being.

We're going to look into attitude, habits, hacks, and practical steps you can take to squeeze as much productivity out of you as possible without making you crazy. They're the ABCs of success.

If you want to be a successful writer, you have to be productive. It's that simple.

So get ready to learn some cool things and be open to making adjustments in your attitude and schedule and habits.

I believe most every writer can become a productive one and that being productive brings great rewards. We feel a wonderful sense of accomplishment when we publish a book and send it out into the world to readers. But we feel an even greater satisfaction when we crank those books out and repeatedly thrill our audience that is eagerly awaiting our next masterpiece.

I don't want to ignore this one important point, though: some writers have huge challenges. Some suffer from chronic illness. Some are caring full-time for a loved one. Some have mental challenges. While it's possible a writer with tough challenges might never crank out books, there are ways for her to at least be more productive during those coveted writing times.

It's not helpful to lay on the guilt if you know you're unable to produce like so many other writers. We should all find joy in our writing, regardless of whether we write ten books or only ten pages a year. However, I believe every writer can benefit from exploring these productivity ABCs. Only know your circumstances and abilities. So take this journey with me and see what works for you.

Ready to get cranking? Let's look at the first big chunk we need to break into grist for the mill: attitude.

*Let's review:*

- *Readers expect a steady flow of books from their favorite authors.*

- *It's important to release books on a regular basis to build fan/reader traction.*

- *If you want to be seen as a career author, you need to crank out books.*

- *Cranking does not mean you churn out junk. Quality cannot be sacrificed.*

- *To be super productive, you need to examine the Productivity ABCs: attitude, biology, and choices.*

- *The objective is to get as much "bang" as possible from each hour of time spent writing.*

- *You have to want to be productive. Motivation is everything.*

- *You don't have to be neurotic or crazy to be super productive.*

- *Every writer, regardless of circumstances and limitations, can utilize ways to be a more productive writer.*

# Chapter 1: Cop an Attitude

Suffice it to say, our attitude affects everything we do. Or don't do. If we have a negative attitude about doing our schoolwork, it won't get done. Or we'll do a hasty, sloppy job. Or we won't be able to concentrate, and it will take three times longer than it should to complete.

We might whip ourselves, pour on the pressure with guilt or threats, and while that might make us get the work done, we will be miserable doing it.

When it comes to writing our books, we certainly don't want it to be a miserable experience. Writing is supposed to be fun! We're supposed to love writing—that's why we long to do it full-time and make it our career.

Sadly, I've met too many career authors who hate writing. Know this—they didn't start out that way. But while they're currently cranking out best sellers year after year, they're not happy campers.

Habits and methods aside (for I believe some are miserable because they don't ever plot, and they stress all the way through writing each book worried they won't make their publisher's deadline), many writers have learned to be productive . . . but at the cost of their joy, and perhaps even their sanity.

## The Goal: Being Happy in Productivity

Maybe that's too obvious to mention—that we don't just want to crank out books; we want to be happy doing so.

But I think it's worth discussing.

Some writers, like me, love the stress of deadlines. I used to work for various newspapers in what was called the Composing Department. That's the department that put the pages of the paper together—oh, long before computer tech invaded the newspaper world.

You know—back when dinosaurs roamed the earth.

Our job in Composing was to print out the newspaper articles on a special paper, use an Xact-O knife to cut out the columns, then run the pieces of paper through the waxer roller (to apply hot liquid wax to the back). From there we'd stick the pieces on the big white tag board pages of the mocked-up edition until every article and ad was in perfect place (the ruler was my best friend). All the while the clock was ticking above our heads and editors were leaning over our shoulders, hurrying us along with press deadline looming.

More than once, I had an editor snatch the big sheet off the work table the second I ran the roller over the last waxed piece, to hurry it over to the camera room. Whew.

But I had fun. I liked the pressure and challenge. And I'm a weird type of person that loves to inflict ridiculous self-imposed deadlines on my projects—because that's what helps me be productive and crank out my books (or blog posts or email blasts).

Here's the thing: I've learned how to be productive and happy doing so because I've taken the time to do the analysis. Which is what you're going to be able to do after going through these chapters.

I've analyzed my personality, my habits, my attitudes, the ways I self-sabotage, the types of excuses I make, the hacks that work (to get me crashing through my obstacles) and don't work, my biology, my eating and drinking preferences . . . and more.

And after analyzing all this stuff that makes up the picture of who I am and how I function each day, it became super clear to me how to be highly productive—and still stay happy.

In fact, all this analysis didn't just help me keep my joy of writing; it elevated it.

## Productivity Must Have a Foundation of Proficiency

I mentioned how satisfying it is to publish a book. Think, then, how fun and exciting it would be to publish three or four books a year. Great books. Ones readers love.

Of course, part of that success—a big part—is reliant on your skill and application of the hard work and time put into mastering your writing craft. But we're not delving into those deep waters in our look at productivity. Let's just assume you *have* been putting in the hard work to become an excellent writer. And in order to be highly productive, that's a must. If you don't master the skills of your craft, you can't produce great books on a regular basis.

Let's just stop here for a second.

A big reason so many aspiring writers aren't productive is they haven't mastered the skills needed. It's no wonder they can't finish that first (or third) novel. Or that memoir or self-help book.

If you're standing in front of a machine that makes door handles or micro circuits—anything, really—and you don't know how to operate the darn thing, nothing is going to happen. You won't produce anything. Those little parts won't come marching down the assembly line conveyor belt.

So, while you may not be ready to produce a line of books because you haven't gotten your chops yet, reading this material on how to be productive is going to help you *immensely*.

Why? Because you can apply everything you learn here to your *pursuit* of mastering your craft.

## Productivity and Life in General

It's the same with anything we attempt in life. You need to learn how to be productive in the pursuit of any goal. You want to learn how to sew your own clothes? Turn your ugly yard into a beautiful and bountiful vegetable garden? All these tips will help you be productive in reaching your goal.

So while this information is geared to writers cranking out books, I hope you'll see how you can apply all of this to life in general. To everything you take on in your life.

It's the tweak on the old adage: writer, know thyself. When you understand yourself—your attitudes and motivation and biology—you can make wise and practical decisions and choices that will impact your success in a positive way.

Don't you want to be productive and successful in everything you do? I do. And I want to make the best use of my time, which is a precious limited resource in our lives. I want every minute to count, but I also want to live a balanced life, free from *unhealthy* stress (I qualify that because I believe some stress is great for us), with my priorities straight.

Each of us has a different order and set of priorities, and you know yours. So keep those in mind as you go through the steps to becoming a highly productive writer. For you, it might mean writing one book a year. With your limitations of schedule, health, or responsibilities, that may equate to huge productivity to you. Don't compare yourself to others, but don't allow lame excuses keep you from reaching those goals.

## Productivity as a Way of Being

Productivity isn't just about getting a lot of stuff done in a (relatively) short period of time. It isn't just about getting something done faster than most people do. Rather than measure productivity in time increments, start thinking about productivity as a way of being, a mind-set.

That's the first shift in attitude I'd like to explore. The "A" in the Productivity ABCs.

Consider this: you could be doing "less" and yet be more productive than previously.

In other words, the effort you are putting out is producing more/better results per minute. Isn't that a primary goal when we talk about ramping up our productivity?

What does "being more productive" look like to you?

While some may think getting the best tools and techniques and tips are the key to super productivity, why is it, then, that getting those things doesn't give them the results they'd hoped for?

Just having a lot of tips and tools in front of you doesn't ensure they'll work for you.

Sometimes these tips and tools aren't easily applied, or they don't fit right into our personalities or lives (or both). Some writers have read a hundred books on the craft, gone to countless workshops and conferences, and taken online courses. But they still aren't producing.

To increase productivity, you have to go deeper, inward.

One big issue, which I'll expound upon in depth later, is self-sabotage. We are usually the biggest thing in our own way. We may blame family, friends, workload, and the cosmos for why we can't be productive. But have you ever heard the saying: "If you want to get something done, ask a busy person to do it"?

Why is that truth? Because busy people, who are already overcommitted, somehow can get even more done. They can be super productive despite the demands on their life. (But be aware that just being *busy* doesn't necessarily mean you're highly producing.)

In other words, they don't make excuses. They don't say "Oh, I can't because . . ."

That's not to say we shouldn't say no when needed. We have to keep balanced and our priorities straight. The worst thing we can do in our effort to be super productive is neglect our responsibilities to the detriment to our family and our health. Saying no is often the best choice.

Sometimes that means getting lost. Don't be so available to everyone. Find places to hide from others, if need be.

This is what this whole big exploration of productivity centers on: achieving our goals while maintaining our joy and balance. So our lives are fulfilling and joyous and productive in a healthy way (physically and emotionally).

So, first thing we often need to do to become super productive is to move out of our own way. Instead of complaining about why we can't get that book written, pointing fingers at people or situations, we need to take a look at ourselves.

Do you make excuses? How many times during a day do you say, "I can't find time to write because I have this to do"? Your excuse might be valid, but I'm guessing most of the time it's not. It's an avoidance technique.

If you say you never have any time at all to write, do you spend time playing games on your phone or computer during the day? How much time? Do you find yourself surfing the Net or scanning through pages of news articles throughout the day? Flipping channels in the evenings searching for something to watch?

Really, I don't have to tell you how much time we all spend (waste) doing things that we really don't have to do. Sure, I play a couple of games on my phone in the evening, after I've put in a long day working on my computer. It clears my mind in some odd way, and it unwinds me so I can get to sleep. That's one of my habits that helps me be productive (and we'll go into the topic of habits further on).

And that's a valid excuse. I'm not sitting there on the couch with the NBA playing in the background (because I have to see if the Warriors are going to win by thirty points again) because I'm procrastinating about writing.

I know you know the difference.

### Excuses, Excuses

So take a look at your valid excuses for not writing. And don't say "I work full-time." Seriously, that is the lamest excuse ever—pardon me for offending you, if I've done so. But countless productive writers work full-time doing something other than writing (a job or homeschooling kids or volunteer work—whatever). Another saying of full of truth: "You always find the time to do the things you love."

You do. You can. You will, if you make up your mind to stop making excuses.

What I believe is that we often make excuses because we can't stir up the motivation to write. Honestly, writing is daunting. It takes intense focus. Sometimes we just don't wanna put that effort out.

Fine. You can either push yourself to write when you don't want to and write garbage, or you can find a hack around your attitude and write well. Before you can come up with useful hacks (workarounds) to your bad attitude, you need to do some self-examination.

Seriously, do you want to be a writer? A successful, productive writer? Then take a look at your excuses and stop making them. First off, at least identify them.

## Authors Who Stopped Making Excuses

Author David Estes quit a job he hated in order to pursue writing full-time, and he now lives in a tropical paradise. Estes didn't expect any of that to happen. He spent ten years working as an accountant/operational risk officer.

When Estes's wife began encouraging him to write, he decided he'd try to write one novel. Almost six years later, he'd written twenty-eight books and published twenty-three of them.

He says, "While I was still working full-time, I was writing two solid hours every day. After my wife and I left our corporate jobs, I continued to write about two to three hours a day, so that didn't change much. More importantly, I was able to focus more on the marketing side of things, which is what really helped me to break through. As far as my 'secret,' it really just comes down to commitment—to my stories, to my characters, to a dream, and to my readers, both present and future. I have so many stories I want to tell, so many characters waiting for their chance to come alive in the pages of my books, and I don't want any of them to get lost in the netherworld of untold stories."

People told Bethany Claire that she couldn't make a living as a writer.

So, when a successful romance novelist told her during a college writing workshop that her manuscript was ready for publication, Bethany just set it aside and kept working on her teaching degree.

"Right in the middle of [a school] lecture, I just quietly got up and marched myself to the registrar's office, where I withdrew from the university on the spot," she says.

Bethany threw herself into learning all she could about the publishing industry. She attended the Romance Writers of America conference and left with the belief that she could make a living as a writer—and with the knowledge of what she'd need. "One piece of advice that every single successful author said was 'write a series,' so the one book I had completed quickly became Book 1 of my Morna's Legacy Series."

In May 2014, about a year after her big leap, Bethany landed on the USA Today best-seller list, and her momentum hasn't stopped.

She currently has seven novels, two novellas, two box sets, and five audiobooks out, with plans for more next spring. "It requires hard, hard work—much more than the normal forty-hour workweek. It requires focus and drive and the refusal to fail, but I can truly say that I love everything about my job, and I know how fortunate I am to be able to say so."

I have a friend who works full-time as an attorney in San Francisco. He has a family (which includes a special-needs child). He commutes on the BART (local rapid transit train) one hour to work and back five days a week. I'm not sure if he still does this, but when he was publishing two novels a year, he spent that commute time on his computer writing his scenes. One hour on the way to work in the morning. One hour on the way home. That's the only time he wrote—because he had other responsibilities, and he knew how to manage his time to lead a balanced happy life and not destroy his joy or his family.

Is he more naturally productive than other writers? More determined or diligent? Maybe he just has the type of personality that can handle a heavy load and lots of stress and hold it together.

Maybe. Maybe not. But what I'll venture to say is this: he took the time to analyze his life, his biology (which we'll get into in later chapters), his personality, and his habits, then figured out the best way to be a productive writer . . . because *he wanted to crank out those novels.*

You see, you have to think hard about what you want. Do you really, truly want to be productive? Or are you just saying that? Is it just about the dream, the enticing picture in your head, of what that successful career looks like to you?

Because if you don't really want to get there, you may be making a lot of excuses for why you are watching reruns of *Castle* every night instead of writing a scene in your novel.

## Just Do It

I've written a lot about procrastination (and if you feel those posts would be helpful for you at this stage, go to Live Write Thrive and search for them by typing *procrastination* in the search bar) because it's easy for me to procrastinate. Me—the super-productive writer who puts out numerous books and hundreds of blog posts and email blasts a year (not to mention online courses and charts and worksheets)—a huge procrastinator.

And one key thing I've learned about procrastination is it won't go away all by its lonesome. Ignoring your excuses won't make them disappear. Every time you think about sitting down to write, that excuse is going to pop up. Or some other one ("Wow, I can see how dirty the floor is—I better get the mop"). Why? Because you haven't learned the technique of getting out of your own way.

You are standing on the narrow path to productivity, high walls on either side, and there's this person blocking you. You can't get past. So you throw up your hands and say, "What's the use?" Then you turn, head down, sulking, and amble back to whatever hole you came out of.

You have to change the picture. Instead, face yourself down and say no. "Get out of my way." Push yourself aside, squeeze by. "Just do it" as the saying goes. Or, to quote Yoda: "There is no *try. Do.*"

This is an attitude shift. It's hard. But if you are in your own way, no one is going to move you to the side but you.

# Change the Way You Talk to Yourself

Here's the thing. Your mind-set is the key. You can't be your own enemy, because then you'll just argue and fight with yourself and never get anywhere.

Ever try to lose weight? If so, you know what I mean. I am always trying to lose ten pounds. It's the story of my life. It's a fight every step of the way. I try meanness, bribery, encouragement—all kinds of methods to psyche myself into not eating that chocolate bar. I am always in an adversarial position with myself when it comes to dieting, and I usually lose because of it.

However, on those rare occasions when I've changed my attitude to a positive one ("You can do it. See, you went all day without cheating!"), I've seen success.

No one's saying this is easy. Habits and deeply ingrained attitudes about self are very hard to change. But the first step toward change is in *looking at the way we talk to ourselves*. And then changing the negative talk into positive talk.

If my commuter friend had said to himself, "I just can't do this. I can't concentrate enough on the BART to write a good scene," then he would have given up before trying. Or partway through trying.

I used to be unable to write a thing if my space wasn't completely quiet. This was a real problem! I could not write a word if any noise could be heard: a clock ticking, someone talking fifty yards away, music playing. This issue really impacted my creativity because I was easily distracted and lost focus.

But I was determined to get writing done those times I was stuck at the doctor's office or Starbucks while waiting all day for my car to be serviced. I needed to overcome this. I needed to change my mind-set. I had to start changing the script and talking to myself differently.

Instead of making excuses ("I just can't work with this noise . . ."), I took on The Little Engine That Could mentality: "I think I can, I think I can . . ." At the end of the book, when the train makes it to the top of the hill, it says, "I thought I could, I thought I could . . ."

I knew it would be hard, and I didn't know if I would succeed, but I was determined to try. Little by little, I started being able to tune out the sounds around me. Sometimes I used headphones and played white noise, which helped a little. But it was my mind-set that won out.

Now, I can write and edit just about anywhere with any noise around me. Well, maybe not if people are screaming. But I've become a more productive writer because I worked on my attitude, faced my excuses, and changed the way I talked to myself. You can do this too.

## Productive People Think Positively

So the first step to becoming a super-productive writer is taking a look at what is stopping you from getting there. Realize that being productive is a state of being, a mind-set, and face down your excuses so you can change the way you talk to yourself (talk yourself out of writing).

Many writers I know have to write because they have publishing deadlines. That forces them to be productive. But many of them hate the deadlines and end up losing their joy in writing. They often write stuff they hate because of their deadline.

I don't like deadlines other than the ones I impose on myself (and I think it's because I know I can ditch the deadline if I truly want to; I have the key to the exit door).

Productive people think differently than unproductive people. You need to challenge yourself and develop that productive mind-set. I'm going to talk next about those habits of productive people, but for now, consider this.

A productive person doesn't say, "Oh, I have too much to do. I'm so stressed, I can't think straight. I wish this were different or I didn't have to . . ."

Here's the way a productive person thinks:

"I need to do this, this, and that. I'd like to get them done by this date. What do I need to change or reschedule so I can get these things done? In what order? What do I need to research before I can start?"

The words we speak to ourselves either motivate and empower us or they paralyze and discourage us. We can either add or reduce stress by the way we talk to ourselves. This applies to every aspect of our lives, not just our writing.

Be your own best friend, not your worst enemy. Work on speaking positive into your life instead of negative.

## Monitoring Your Self-Talk Is the First Step

If you have a mind-set of failure, you're going to fail.

I can't address this specific topic in depth in this discussion on productivity. So if you have a real problem with your attitude—if you're often negative and wading through oceans of self-recrimination and feelings of failure—you'll probably need more than a regular pep talk about adopting a positive attitude.

But in general, observing and catching yourself when thinking in negative ways is the first step toward change. Identify the negative self-talk and switch it out with positive, practical, and proactive statements. That's how you thwart all the slings and arrows you throw at yourself.

I hope you can see that before you can tackle just about any issue related to productivity, you have to look at your attitude. If you are making excuses and thinking negatively about your writing goals, you aren't going to get anywhere. You have to want that dream you see in your head.

How much do you want it? Only you can answer that.

And I believe that if you can honestly say you want it and are willing to work for it, you can get there by applying all the things you'll be learning in this book.

For now, ask yourself this one question: What one thing could I change right now that would have the biggest impact on my productivity?

Just one thing.

Write this down, think about why this is your biggest obstacle, and how you might change your self-talk about it, stop making excuses, and push it aside enough to get past yourself and closer to becoming a super-productive writer.

*Let's review:*

- *Writing should be fun! Our attitude about writing affects our joy.*

- *You have to analyze your personality and attitudes and be willing to make tweaks.*

- *Before you can become highly productive, you must get to a level of proficiency in your writing chops.*

- *Productivity is a way of being and will seep into all areas of your life. Learning to be a super-productive writer will help you be productive in all you do.*

- *Productivity isn't about relying on technique, tools, or tips. It's about looking inside and "knowing" ourselves.*

- *We have to be honest and look at our excuses as to why we aren't getting the writing done.*

- *Procrastination doesn't go away by itself. You have to take proactive steps to blast through it.*

- *You have to change the way you talk to yourself. Monitor your self-talk and turn the negative thinking into positive thinking.*

# Chapter 2: The Power of Positive Thinking

Yeah, we've all heard it before: the power of positive thinking. It's so overused an expression, it's corny. But we're going there.

You can become that productive, resilient author by training your brain to stay positive when circumstances around you are seeking to drag you under. Learning to conquer challenges and threat of failure is an essential skill.

We have a bias toward remembering our failures and forgetting our successes. In one sense, that's good for us, because we can learn from failure and improve. On the other hand, dwelling on our failures stymies productivity. Best-case scenario is that we learn to view our failures in a positive light.

I love what Thomas Edison said: "I have not failed 10,000 times. I have not failed once. I have succeeded in proving that those 10,000 ways will not work. When I have eliminated the ways that will not work, I will find the way that will work."

Because he had that positive attitude, he kept trying. If he hadn't, we might all be writing with pen and paper by the light of a candle.

"If I've learned anything through all of this, it's that each day is a canvas waiting to be painted," said Craig Sager, who, at the time of my writing this, just died yesterday. He was a much-loved sports announcer who always seemed to be cheerful and happy. Even during the last years in his struggle to beat his leukemia, in the news reports I saw him in, he still kept that same smile and upbeat manner. His positivity influenced and inspired countless numbers of people.

It takes a determined mind-set not to succumb to despair and negativity when life throws curve balls at us. But even in the best of times, some of us can't help but slip into negativity instead of counting our blessings.

Author Jessica McBrayer could have given up her writing dream, and no one would have faulted her. She's a prolific author who's published eleven paranormal novels. But right before her first novel was published, her daughter died.

"I had just published my first book two weeks before she died," she says in an interview. "She was so proud of me. I'm not going to tell you that I used the grief to fuel my writing or to get through it because I did the opposite. I shut down. I couldn't look at my computer. I was just devastated.

"But something amazing happened when I came out of the fog and started to write again. I found myself creating a character that was based on my daughter. It surprised and delighted me when I figured out what I had done. I used that character throughout my entire series. She was one of my favorites, of course, and even got her own novellas. The fans love her too.

"I think anyone that creates—sculptors, writers, painters, photographers—will agree that hard work is essential. But that doesn't mean we can't love our job. We may set our own hours, but we put our blood, sweat, and tears into that time. I love my job, but it is work."

We can all learn a lot from Jessica's positive attitude.


## Gratitude Is the Best Attitude

You might say that being grateful for your health and your nice car doesn't impact your productivity. And you're right—as far as it impacts directly. But if you take on a grateful attitude in life, in general, you will think positively, not negatively, of so much around you.

So here are some tips to help you train your brain to ride on the positive railway:

1. *Express gratitude.* As I mentioned above, when you are facing difficulties or hard challenges, thinking about your blessings can balance that bias toward negative thinking. The more you dwell on good things in your life, the more present they will be in your brain and short-term memory. Maybe keep a log or journal in which you write each day a list of the things you are grateful for.

   Consider little things as well as big things. Such as right now, my kitty Thelma is curled up and purring on my lap. She makes me smile as she tries to tuck her head under my armpit. Things that make us smile lighten our hearts and seem to obliterate boulders that block our way to getting a project done. If it makes it any easier, use an app for your iPhone like Day One, or OhLife, a free email-based journal program, to help you do this.

2. *Repeat positive affirmations.* We all know the power of the message. I grew up with the popular book *The Medium is the Massage,* by Marshall McLuhan (yes, that is the correct title, though the result of a typesetter's error), which pounded home how messages can affect us emotionally. The more we tell ourselves positive things (remember what I said about "I think I can, I think I can . . ."?), and the more often we repeat them, the more likely we'll believe them.

   My pastor has a saying: *"Faith* it till you make it." It's not so much we're *faking it*—lying to ourselves. It's more that we are acting in faith—that if we keep telling ourselves we can and will be productive and overcome any obstacle in our way, and then act in faith believing that, we will make it.

It's as if we have to psyche ourselves into believing what's good for us. So choose a few affirmations that will help you where you need it. "I can handle anything that comes my way." "I am perfectly capable of writing a novel in three months." Write them down and stick them next to your computer. Recite them until they become mantras that play in your head throughout the day. This is how we rewire our brain and eliminate the negative recordings we've been playing since childhood.

3. *Challenge those negative thoughts.* Every time your brain derails onto that negative track, separate yourself from it and picture it as something "over there" that you can manipulate. Don't ride that train; pull the track switch and move it onto another set of rails. When you tell yourself "I'm a failure. I'll never get this book written," say instead, "I haven't failed. I'm facing a challenge and I will conquer it. I'm going to try again."

Maybe that attempt was just one way of showing you what won't work. Like Edison's lightbulb. If it took him ten thousand tries to get that invention right, should you complain and give up if your first attempt at a particular scene flopped? Or your effort in rescheduling your job and day care didn't pan out to allow you time to write? I think not.

### Bouncing Back

Positive attitudes have been called "the undo effect" (Barbara Fredrickson, *Positivity*). They help us to quickly recover from negative emotions. When we generate a positive perspective, it helps us bounce back. And that "bouncing back" brings motivation or impetus. Which is what we need to be productive. Wallowing never got a book written.

Think of it this way: negativity is like a vise grip that squeezes and constricts our creativity. Negative emotions such as fear, anger, blame, and resentment narrow our focus in a way that obscures options. Worry, especially, paralyzes us.

We worry our books will get bad reviews. We worry that our plot is stupid. We worry that we'll never sell a copy, so why waste all this time.

Studies were done with highly stressed students about to give speeches. In under a minute, their cardiovascular system relaxed (heart rate down, blood pressure lowered, artery constriction lightened) when these students were shown a movie clip of peaceful ocean waves and puppies frolicking. Other studies show that the more people entertain positive emotions, the quicker they can let go of negative ones.

There are lots of occasions when we need to "bounce back." When something upsets our carefully planned schedule. When relationships invade and bring stress. When world events get us down. I get so discouraged by the news that it drains me of all motivation. If I have projects I want to get done, I have to stop looking at the news. (We'll look hard into distractions in later chapters because that's a curse we are all under!)

So when these things come at us and bog us down, we want to bounce back as quickly as possible. Changing the picture (literally, by looking at uplifting scenery or images) can help us do that.

When you adopt a positive outlook, you are open to processing new information, and your awareness expands. That's what we writers need when trying to come up with scenes and plots and characters.

One researcher determined that we need at least three positive emotions to lift us up in a way to be able to counter every single negative one that drags us down. And these positive emotions don't have to be huge or profound; they can be subtle. They just need to be frequent.

And, of course, the best positive attitude to have is gratitude. When you've learned the secret of how to be content in life, it goes far toward productivity.

I have the entire (full version) of the famous Serenity Prayer pinned to the wall next to my computer. One part of that prayer reads "Living one day at a time; Enjoying one moment at a time; Accepting hardships as the pathway to peace."

Sometimes we feel we must change our situation before we can be positive and plow ahead on our projects. But there are times when we can't change a darn thing. In that case, we can either "accept the things we cannot change" and adopt a positive attitude of gratitude, or we can wallow in the mire of negativity and unproductiveness. Our choice.

## The Attitudes of Successfully Motivated People

Let's take a look at some of the attitudes of super-productive people. Essentially, these attitudes are manifestations of positive thinking. But I'm going to present them in negative terms: in what these successful people *don't do.*

1. *They don't let others' opinions of them affect their joy.* If your sense of self-worth and general mood are greatly affected by others' opinions or treatment of you, you are no longer the master of your happiness. Everyone is different, and some people are more sensitive to criticism or another's bad mood. If you are one of those thin-skinned types, try to work on this.

   Successful productive, self-motivated people feel good about their accomplishments, and they won't allow another's opinion or accomplishment take that from them.

   While it's impossible to turn off your reactions completely, you don't have to compare yourself to others, and you can step back and put a negative comment at arm's length.

When you put your work out for public viewing, you're not going to please everyone. That one-star review is a badge of honor (we all get them—even the most successful authors in the world). Don't be overly sensitive to others' negativity. Rise above it.

2. *They don't demand perfection of themselves.* Successful productive, self-motivated people don't aim to be perfect—because they know such a goal is impossible. We all fail sometimes; that's being human. If you expect perfection, you will always end up with that negative feeling of failure, and you're back to wallowing instead of producing.

This is something I see often. Writers spend years on the same manuscript, lamenting that it's just not right yet. They may have had numerous editors help them, and they've been told they have a great novel. But they can't let go of it. It's not perfect, and the fear of failure prevents them for taking the next big steps (submission or publishing). They are stuck in a rut, and they're certainly not being productive.

Highly productive writers know a book is never going to be perfect. But it can come close. Experience helps a writer determine when good is good enough. I know this with my own books. And once I determine I've done my best and the novel or nonfiction book is worthy of publication, I get it ready and launch it. I won't put out shoddy work—I take pride in everything I publish. Each book has to meet my very high standards. But I know my books aren't perfect and will never be so.

This is such an important factor in becoming a productive writer: learning when done is done and it's time to let it go.

3. *They don't dwell on their failures.* Failure erodes self-confidence—that goes without saying. But I'm saying it anyway, because we need to be reminded. You are going to fail sometimes. Just face it. You'll have books that flop or get some bad reviews. Failure often comes from taking risks, trying something new. Every time you publish a book, you take a risk.

I know one best-selling author (who sells millions of copies of her suspense thrillers) who cries every time she finishes writing a new novel and turns it in to her publisher. She's sure it's the worst thing she's ever written and that it will ruin her career for good. She goes through this with every book (some therapy might help here). Sure, she's highly productive, and what pushes her to be so is her contracted deadlines.

We all have our emotional issues we struggle with—some of us have more or worse ones than others. But successfully productive writers know that their success lies in their ability to keep moving ahead in the face of failure (or possible looming failure). And if they've suffered big failures in the past, they don't dwell on them. They do what the apostle Paul recommends in the Bible book of Philippians: forget the past and press forward to what lies ahead.

4. *They don't dwell on problems.* We've already talked about this a bit. If you dwell on the negative, it hinders your productivity. When you adopt a positive mind-set and focus on actions to better yourself and your circumstances, you will be able to get your best work done. Highly successful people know they're most effective when they focus on solutions.

5. *They won't hang out with people who will pull them down.* While we can't live in a bubble and separate completely from negative people, we can try to limit our associations. Highly productive people surround themselves with others like them. No surprise that a whole lot of productive people are positive and upbeat (most of the time).

When we hang with complainers and those in the throes of a pity party, it's going to drag down our mood. We might feel we're being rude to excuse ourselves from such company, but often it's the healthiest thing (for us and the complainer) to do. You may not want to be rude or callous, but there's a difference between offering a listening ear and being pulled into the mud with them.

6. *They won't say yes unless they really want to.* One thing I've learned about being a productive person is it draws people to me who want favors. Remember that saying: "If you want to get something done, ask a busy person to do it"? Problem with busy, productive people is they sometimes can't say no. They overcommit. And that can cause stress. Saying no is a challenge for most people, I think. But *no* is a word we should all feel comfortable using.

Highly successful people avoid hemming with phrases like "I'm not sure I can" or "I don't know if I have time."

Saying no honors your existing commitments and frees up the time needed to fulfill them. You should never feel guilty for saying no in these situations. Or for disappointing someone because of your decision.

So as you begin to examine your attitudes and see which ones are blocking your path to productivity, keep these points in mind. Work on that positive outlook. Catch yourself when you slip into negativity that keeps you from getting things done. Change the picture and repeat those positive affirmations to flush out the tendency to dwell on the negative.

These are all things that will help you mold the mind-set needed to become a successful, productive writer.

Next, we're going to look at some practical steps you can take to become the kind of writer that can crank out great books. We're going to explore our biology, the "B" in our Productivity ABCs.

*Let's review:*

- *Writers need to train their brains to stay positive about their writing.*

- *Adopting a daily attitude of gratitude will go a long way toward being positive.*

- *Repeating positive affirmations will begin to erase the negative talk tape loop.*

- *Challenge those negative thoughts when they crop up in order to break the pattern.*

- *Positive attitudes help us to "bounce back" quickly.*

- *Super-productive people don't let others spoil their joy.*

- *Super-productive people don't demand perfection of themselves or dwell on their failures.*

- *Super-productive people associate with others that are uplifting and positive.*

- *Super-productive people learn how to say no and only say yes when they want to.*

# Chapter 3: Preparing the Ground for Productivity

Before a farmer plants seeds, he has to prepare the ground. It's hard for seeds to sprout and grow into healthy plants if soil is depleted or rock hard. If you're hoping to grow some beautiful, highly producing vegetables, you must first ensure that soil is perfect for that type of plant.

See, not all plants are created equal when it comes to soil needs. Some plants need acidic base; others need alkaline. Some need the soil very porous, and other do well in claylike ground.

If you plant your seeds in the wrong soil type, they won't sprout. Or if they do, they'll die before they make it to maturity.

You can liken your attitude to soil preparation to some extent. But there are other factors that go into "preparing the ground" for productivity. And so, we need to take time to examine the B in the Productivity ABCs: biology.

Many of those "growth" factors have to do with your biology and personality. Like seeds, every person is different when it comes to biology (or physiology). Your "soil" needs are unique, so instead of following any or all random advice from experts or author friends, you need to spend some time analyzing yourself in order to make some key decisions that will impact your productivity.

For instance, if you're a morning person (*moi*) and really struggle focusing on hard things at three in the afternoon (your natural nap time), and you decide to spend one hour a day—at three p.m.—working on your novel, that's not a great idea. You're not going to be as productive with your effort as you would if you allocated that writing time to eight a.m.

This may be a no-brainer. You may already know when your brain is the sharpest, and you already try to assign time to write to take advantage of those perky gray cells.

But let's take this a step further.

## Calculate Your Biological Prime Time

During the day, your energy fluctuates. This fluctuation is impacted by what you eat and when, how much caffeine or sugar you consume, how tired you are, how hard you work, what type of work you're doing, how much you're using your physical body, and a whole lot more.

Sam Carpenter, in his book *Work the System*, coined the phrase "biological prime time." He suggests charting energy during the day for a few weeks. And not just noting your energy highs and lows between six a.m. and nine p.m. You want to jot down your peak times of focus and lack thereof as well as when those bursts of motivation occur.

You'd want to note when you exercise and for how long, what times you wake up and go to sleep. Basically you keep a journal with the emphasis on energy and concentration. Think about trying this.

When you do this, you can note the variables that affect your energy levels. If you have a couple of beers with lunch and then you have to go take a two-hour nap, you might conclude the alcohol impacted your energy in the afternoon. If you'd hoped to put in a couple of brilliant writing hours between two and four p.m., you might see how those beers weren't a good idea.

To successfully chart your energy levels, here are some recommendations:

1. *Cut out caffeine, alcohol, and all mood enhancers or depressants to get an accurate reading.* Okay, no fun (maybe you'll make it a week instead of three weeks, but go for it), but this is essential if you truly want to get a handle on your biological prime time.

If you are super dependent on caffeine, wait until you've gotten through withdrawal before charting your energy levels (this applies to other drugs as well).

2. *Wake up and go to sleep when you naturally feel like it.* Don't set an alarm. This may not work for everyone—especially those who have to work a 9-5 job or the like. But if you can, do it.

3. *Record your energy levels every hour on the hour.* Make some kind of chart (using Excel, a Google doc, or a scratch pad) and set an alarm on your phone or calendar program to *ding* you every hour. You can come up with your own system. Maybe a 1-10 scale in which 1 is nearly dead ("dragging your sorry body out of bed" kind of dead) and 10 is Superman energy.

In addition to noting your energy, consider having a column(s) for motivation and/or focus. I think it's also helpful to note at the hourly marker when and what you eat or just ate. While some may not consider sugar a factor, I sure do. So think about jotting down when you consume something sweet and how that impacts your energy. You may want to go whole hog here and cut sugar out of your diet to see how that helps you determine your biological prime time (or not). Just a suggestion. I know— giving up caffeine is torture enough.

4. *Collect the data for at least three weeks.* That's what's recommended for best results. The more data, the more helpful, because you'll see a stronger pattern in your energy peaks and valleys.

Once you have this chart all filled out, take a look at the results. You should be able to see interesting patterns and trends in your biology. You'll be able to schedule your writing time based on when you tend to be the most focused, when you have the most energy.

## Make the Needed Adjustments

You may decide to do your exercising when you have the most energy. And if right after that, you seem to have high motivation and focus, that's when you should schedule your writing and/or research time.

Take a look at your energy spikes. Try to analyze what causes them. Usually eating a heavy meal (or too much caffeine and sugar) can cause a sudden energy drop. You might want to adjust the times you eat meals or snacks.

This isn't a hard-and-fast science. Be flexible. But taking the time to understand your own biological patterns and cycles is part of getting to know yourself. Just making minor adjustments in your eating times, sleeping times, or exercise times may make a huge difference in how productive you are with your writing.

I write best between six and nine a.m. I wrote these last two sections of this material right after getting up at six, and it's now seven forty-five. That's about two thousand words. I'm feeling super productive and gearing my brain to get ready to run two miles on my treadmill.

Though that's the last thing I really want to do this morning, I know if I put the run off until the afternoon, I'll drag through it and feel miserable—because I know my energy for exercising peaks in the morning and all but vanishes in the afternoon. Regardless of what I eat during the day.

I know these things about myself, and so I have learned to adjust to my biological prime time and plan my schedule accordingly.

Try this and see what results.

See if you learn some insightful things about your biology that help you become a more productive writer.

Instead of being hard on yourself, pushing yourself to write at times when you just can't work up the energy or motivation, be your own best friend and, with that positive attitude, sit down to write at the best time for you.

## Make the Best with What You Have

Of course, not all of us have the freedom of schedule to align our writing perfectly with our biology. Some writers have other jobs and commitments. Some have small kids in the house and have to find writing time between dropping them off at school and picking them up and taking them to soccer practice.

Even with schedule restraints and demands, if you take the time to assess the peaks and valleys of your energy, motivation, and focus, you should be able to tweak some activities in your daily life to make room for highly productive writing time. It may not be easy, but at least, with this information about your biology, you'll have a road map to productivity.

Perhaps, over time, you can rearrange your schedule even more.

Think about setting up carpools in order to take turns with other parents driving to soccer practice. Or bring your laptop to the practice and work while the kids are running back and forth across the field. Maybe get up an hour earlier to write or get other tasks done that will free up an hour or two in the afternoon, when you've found your energy level is at its highest.

I've said this before, and it won't be the last time: you gotta want to be a highly productive writer. If you don't, all the energy and focus in the world won't help.

And if you're committed to that career you dream of, don't make excuses. You may need to cut back on the coffee. You may need to take that half-hour power nap each day.

Do everything you can to adjust and streamline your life to make this happen. It's not neurotic! It's sensible.

## When Your Energy Drops

So what should you do at those times when your energy sags?

1. *Recharge.* Yep, those power naps are the thing. Don't knock them or feel guilty about them. Michael Hyatt says one of his most popular posts on his blog is about taking power naps (yes, he takes naps). It's a great post. He lists lots of famous nappers, such as da Vinci, Einstein, Edison, Ronald Regan, Eleanor Roosevelt, and Rockefeller. Suffice it to say, napping recharges our bodies and brains. I've found that even though I'm not at my peak in the afternoons, if I take a short nap, I've been able to do some highly productive writing afterward, much to my surprise.

   In addition, if you're on an "energy roll," why stop and take a lunch break (which will interrupt the flow and perhaps give you an energy drop)?

2. *Do low-energy activities.* If you're sluggish in the mornings, get those low-energy tasks out of the way. Load the dishes in the dishwasher. Get through your email. Do some reading.

3. *Boost your energy.* If you need to keep going and stay productive, think about that coffee, green tea, or chocolate bar. While those may give you a brief energy spike, that might be what you need right then. Don't rely on these things to get you through hours and hours, though. You know as well as I do that, in the long run, this is not going to be great for your body or overall health.

4. *Watch what you eat.* Those energy dips are often caused by those "bad" foods. So be aware of that. You may be creating a lot of those energy dips—ones you'd be better off without.

Here's one great byproduct to assessing your ideal writing times based on your natural energy levels: you don't have to feel guilty when you can't seem to get any work done during those low-energy times. If you can't write in the evenings, don't. If that's the only time you have to write, be considerate of yourself and don't lay on the pressure or guilt trips. Know that you may not get a whole lot done, and pat yourself on the back for what you do get done.

Just as with my adjusting to writing in a noisy environment over time, you may find that if you do push through working during those low-energy times, eventually you'll make them more productive.

Interestingly, in response to a survey I sent out to numerous super-productive writers, *every single one of them* said their writing routine optimizes the time of day they feel most focused and energetic.

I've learned to focus and write at three in the morning and three in the afternoon. Sometimes I need to get the writing done, and I don't have the luxury of writing at my peak times. I may not get as much done as I hope, but I do get something of worth on the page. Many of the novels I've published have been written mostly during my "off" hours.

Again, a lot of this is attitude (adjusting your mind-set, thinking positively, being nice to yourself, etc.). But I hope you're starting to see that becoming a highly productive writer is so much more than attitude.

*Let's review:*

- *Attitude isn't the only factor affecting productivity. We have to examine and understand our biology, then work with our nature for best results.*

- *Our energy fluctuates during the day, and various factors affect it. So we must look at those factors and see which are draining or helping our energy.*

- *Taking the time to calculate your "biological prime time" will give you the info you need to make adjustments to your life and schedule to be super productive.*

- *Analyze what drains your energy and motivation and see if you can eliminate or change something to avoid that.*

- *Determine when your best times are to write, exercise, eat, and other routine activities.*

- *You have to combine attitude with biology. All the energy and focus in the world won't make you productive if your attitude isn't helping.*

- *When your energy sags, take a nap, boost your energy, or switch to low-energy activities.*

- *Watch what you eat and adjust your eating habits if they cause your energy to dip often.*

- *Understanding your biology will help you to not feel guilty if you can't be productive at certain times.*

# Chapter 4: Functioning at Your Peak

Let's go a bit further in this exploration of biology, the "B" in our Productivity ABCs (along with attitude and choices). We looked at how we can derive our prime biological time for writing, and we've seen some ways we can make adjustments in our routines for greater productivity.

But there's so much more to examine.

So let's look at some other factors that can influence our productivity, and these have to do with ensuring we function at our peak performance level.

Basic body needs have to be met, and often we neglect these.

1. *Get enough sleep.* If you're like me, and maybe most adults, you overrate sleep. It's a waste of time, right? I mean, should we really spend one-third of our life checked out? I wish we didn't ever have to sleep. Why not just a half-hour power nap a day to call it good?

   Wishful thinking aside, we have to accept that we need sleep. Sleep deprivation leads to low productivity. Without that good night's sleep, our brains can feel foggy and unfocused. That cup of coffee may seem to wake us up, but it's an illusion.

   Good sleep improves our ability to think clearly, retain information, control our emotions and behavior, and stay alert. Sleep refreshes the brain so that when we tackle our tasks, we have that energy and concentration that's needed. So don't neglect your sleep (more on this later).

2. *Drink lemon water.* Or water with some other fruit in it. This is a great substitution for coffee. Lemons and other citrus have great energy-boosting properties with no bad side effects. Some people prefer green tea for this reason (I drink a decaf green tea since I can't have drinks with caffeine). Consider hot water with lemon and honey if you're cold. It will hydrate your lymph system.

   Lemon water is also antibacterial, antiviral, and immune-boosting. It can rid you of headaches, improve your digestion, and reduce acidity in the body. And, best of all, it increases cognitive capacity and improves mood, helping you on your way to that peak productive zone.

3. *Exercise daily.* If you're like me, you feel exercise is the worst waste of time. Granted, I love to hike, and I'll do "power hikes" to get my heart rate up. But often I'll be sitting at my computer thinking how I need to head out to my yoga class or put in my two-mile run. There is never a time during the day when I want to exercise instead of writing or working on something pressing in my schedule. I'd rather scrub the toilet. But I make myself do it because I know that my writing and writing productivity are dependent on my good health.

   When we exercise regularly, we have more energy overall. We sleep better. We feel better. We have a more positive attitude about ourselves, and that spills over into other areas of our life.

   Some writers have found a way to write while walking on a treadmill. That's on my list of things to try.

   Exercise reduces stress, and we sure have more than enough stress in our lives. It stimulates growth of new brain cells, which improves overall brain function. Those new brain cells allow you to be more efficient, think clearly, and learn faster.

4. *Work to develop healthy, supportive relationships.* Healthy, loving relationships increase our happiness and success. We're social beings, and often writing is a solitary activity. We have to "get out of our cage" regularly and interact with people in the real sense. I mean, more than popping onto Facebook or Twitter and engaging in some brief chats.

   I live out in the country, and I don't have any close friends nearby. So I usually head to town a half-hour away and write and work out at my local rec center. I'll spend a day at Starbucks or the library just to interact with people (and to people-watch).

   But while that kind of social interacting can help us keep from wallowing in isolation, we really need deeper, more meaningful relationships with others to keep us sane and positive, so we can be productive in our writing and all our endeavors. It takes time and effort to grow personal relationships, and choosing people who are uplifting and positive will help us be the same way.

   A strong social network decreases stress and gives us a sense of belonging. We feel exalted, elevated, and encouraged to live out our dreams—and we can do the same for our writer friends. Conversely, immersing ourselves among those who are negative and unproductive can drag us down.

5. *Be optimistic.* We've been looking at the effects of positive thinking on our productivity. Some people are naturally optimistic (those "the glass is half full" types). Others not so much. If you're not usually optimistic, you need to change the way you talk to yourself (as discussed earlier in this book). You need to take responsibility for how you think and feel. Blaming others is a dead end.

Remember those positive affirmations? Write them down and say them to yourself throughout the day. Taking responsibility for your own happiness is empowering. And when bad things happen, don't blame yourself.

Look for the best in every situation. Find ways to turn the negative into positive. A positive outlook strengthens your immunes system and gives you the resilience to face fear and challenges.

6. *Spend some time alone.* It's hard to be a writer who hates being alone. Since writing is usually a solitary pursuit, we often want to spend our non-writing time in the company of others. However, going off somewhere alone—on a walk, for instance—is great for generating peace of mind and getting centered.

I'm grateful for my big black lab because he always pressures me to take him on a walk (like, every hour). While I often get annoyed, because I'm in the middle of being "highly productive," I know that walk is just what I need. I'd made it such a daily routine that my former dog, Sweetie, always knew when noon rolled around. About one minute before twelve, she'd come over to me at the computer and start pushing her nose into my hand. She had an alarm clock in her brain—every day she did this at the exact same time.

Spending time alone recharges you. It clears your head, giving you permission to wholly unplug from work and commitments and being social.

While you might want to sit somewhere outside and close your eyes, listen to the birds or the sounds of traffic (depending on where you live or work), I prefer walking. The rhythm of movement works wonders on my body and brain. Hiking is one of my favorite pastimes for that reason.

During those alone times, we can be in the here and now. We can spend time in self-reflection. Get perspective on our life. We can problem-solve and plan our week. It's one of the best things we can do to make the rest of our day productive.

These are some of the best ways to function at your peak, but I think getting a good night's sleep is perhaps the most important, so let's take a deeper look at the role sleep plays in being super productive.

*Let's review:*

- *Many factors can impact your productivity, so try to adopt some habits to help you improve.*

- *Getting enough sleep is crucial to being clear-headed and productive.*

- *Drink lemon water or green tea—or something other than coffee that can help you focus and function well.*

- *Try to develop and maintain positive, healthy relationships with those around you.*

- *Adopting an optimistic attitude can affect your biology (energy, concentration).*

- *Spending quiet time alone to recharge is tremendously helpful for productivity.*

# Chapter 5: To Sleep Perchance to Write

Some people say they'll sleep when they're dead; they can't bother to sleep right now. Too much to do. Too many books waiting to be written. And they're not going to get written while they're sleeping.

For those of us (yes, I'm one of them) who feel sleep should be phased out, ignoring the need for sleep is going to make us "dead" sooner than later. Pushing hard without sleep for long periods of time is bad for our health. And worse (as far as some of us are concerned)—it's a productivity killer.

Studies show that the short-term productivity that results from skipping sleep is negated by the detrimental effects on our mood, ability to focus, and access to high brain function for days that follow. Even drunk people can sometimes outperform those who are sleep-deprived.

New research shows that when you sleep, your brain actually removes toxic proteins from its neurons, and this can only occur when you're asleep. It's like our brains offload bad stuff while we're konked out, sneaking it out the back door, so to speak. If we don't get enough sleep, those toxic proteins build up, wreaking havoc in our heads and impairing our ability to think clearly. And, no, coffee won't fix this problem.

## Why Sleep Deprivation Is Bad for Your Health

Sleep deprivation kills your concentration and creativity. But it also causes more damage than that.

It's been linked to heart attacks, strokes, type 2 diabetes, and obesity. Sleep deprivation stresses you because it triggers the body to overproduce cortisol. Cortisol can bring about negative side effects, weaken your immune system, and make you look older (because cortisol breaks down skin collagen). And in men (sorry, guys!), lack of proper sleep reduces testosterone levels and lowers sperm count.

Numerous studies show that people who get enough sleep live longer, healthier lives. If that's not enough for you to think twice about cheating yourself on sleep, lack of sleep compromises your body's ability to metabolize carbs and control food intake. When you sleep less, you eat more and have a harder time burning those calories. So sleep deprivation can make you fat!

Going without sleep makes you hungrier by increasing the appetite-stimulating hormone ghrelin and reduces the levels of the hormone leptin, which helps you feel satiated.

People who sleep less than six hours a night are 30% more likely to become obese than those who sleep seven to nine hours a night (though, no guarantees, of course. And don't use those long hours of sleep to justify overeating!).

## So How Much Sleep Do We Really Need?

Those seven to nine hours are usually enough to do the trick. Few people function at their best with fewer hours, though some need more. A recent survey of top CEOs found that less than half get a minimum of six hours of sleep each night. As do one-third of all US workers. It's estimated that sleep deprivation accounts for more than $63 billion annually in lost productivity.

So this is a real problem in our fast-paced, work-mentality society.

## What You Can Do

It's not just about how much you sleep that matters. It's how you sleep. One way to ensure your sleep is sound is to be aware of "sleep killers."

Here are some things that kill sleep. If you can avoid all or most of them, the quality of your sleep should improve, if you've been struggling with getting a good night's sleep.

- *Don't do drugs.* Any drugs that might sedate you: alcohol, Nyquil, Valium, Ambien, and the like. It goes without saying that these drugs disrupt your brain's natural sleep process. Our sleep goes through different stages at different times. And while we might not understand why we shift through five stages in cycles, clearly there's a biological reason. And when we interrupt that cycle of about 90-110 minutes (especially on a regular basis), we throw our brain into a sort of chaos.

  What happens if you don't reach your sleep REM (rapid eye movement) stage? Though studies conflict some, it's thought that problems may occur in cognition and pain sensitivity. Lack of rapid-eye-movement sleep may interfere with long-term memory. Rats deprived of REM sleep experienced reduced cell proliferation in the part of the brain associated with long-term memory. Reduced REM sleep may contribute to weight problems in teenagers and children. You may be more sensitive to pain without enough sleep, and coping skills and reflexes may diminish.

- *Stop drinking caffeine-loaded drinks after noon.* Most people know that coffee and other caffeine-packed drinks keep you awake. That's why a lot of people drink them. But caffeine interferes with sleep by increasing adrenaline production and blocking sleep-inducing chemicals in the brain. Caffeine has a half-life of six hours, which means it takes a full twenty-four hours to pass from your body. If you drink a cup of coffee at eight a.m., you'll still have 25% of the stuff in your body at eight p.m. Anything you drink at noon will still be at 50% strength when you go to bed (sometime before midnight).

And when you do finally drop off, your sleep is disrupted at the essential REM stage. You'll start the next day with a cognitive handicap, and to counteract that, you'll reach for that cup of coffee . . . and begin the whole off-kilter process again.

- *Avoid Blue Light Waves.* Short-wavelength blue light affects our mood, energy level, and sleep. We get high concentrations of blue light from the sun in the morning, and that light helps us wake up by halting the production of melatonin (which makes you sleepy). So the blue light helps you feel alert. Morning sunlight can improve your mood and energy, but you can replicate the effect by turning on a lamp with strong blue light wavelengths.

  In the afternoon, those wavelengths wane in natural light, so that, by the evening, your brain signals you to become sleepy. Problem is, most electronic devices emit blue light, and they do so brightly and in your face. When you confuse your brain by constantly exposing it to blue light when it's "not supposed" to experience it, it can derail your natural sleep processes, even long after you turn off your device. It's recommended by some that if you are going to work on a computer or pad or phone in the evenings, you should limit your exposure with a filter or some protective eyewear.

  I'm thinking that's a strong possibility for why I have such trouble falling asleep; I work on devices right up until bedtime. Even Kindle Paperwhites give off blue light, so if you like to read yourself to sleep, you might want to consider the old-fashioned way of doing so—with paperback or hardcover book in hand.

- *Don't have an erratic wake-up schedule.* Consistency is key to a good night's sleep, and waking up at the same time every day improves mood and sleep quality by regulating that circadian rhythm. Our brains acclimate to routine and so will move through those sleep cycles more smoothly. About an hour before you wake, hormone levels increase gradually, along with body temperature and blood pressure, so that you grow more alert. Ever wake up a few seconds before your alarm goes off? This is why, especially if you follow the same schedule much of the time.

Back in the day, the sun woke us up gradually. Picture that slow shift from darkness to light, from no blue light to full-on blue light. I sleep next to my window, and I can sense when dawn is coming. I tend to wake up right before that, my body knowing morning is approaching. We were made to gradually wake along with the light of day. But many of us work erratic schedules and depend on an alarm to jolt us awake. No wonder our brains are tired and confused.

- *Don't "binge sleep" on your days off.* Sleeping in on your days off is actually counterproductive to "catching up" on your sleep. It messes with your established rhythm. As a result, you'll often feel groggy and tired and unable to concentrate on much. Maybe that's fine to you because you want to kick back and relax. But you're not doing yourself any real favors—especially if you're hoping to get some serious writing in on your days off work.

- *Don't let others tell you how much sleep you personally need.* Just because someone tells you eight hours is ideal, it may not be your ideal. I know, for myself, my need for sleep varies greatly at different times of the year. As soon as fall comes around (and that natural blue light from the sun decreases), I get super sleepy. I need to take afternoon naps, and I go to bed earlier. Animals hibernate, so it's not surprising that we lean toward needing more sleep in the winter.

For the most part, people sleep less than they need to, and they're underperforming because of it. Though it may seem counterintuitive, sometimes the more sleep you get, the more you can produce. That's because the time you spend being productive is quality, unimpaired time. Without enough sleep, it may take you three times as long to write a chapter in your book that's half as good as what you might write after a full night's sleep.

- *Stop working once evening rolls around.* Oh, I'm bad at this. I often try to get in an hour or so of work—on my blue-light-saturated computer—before bedtime, after I've watched a couple of NBA games on TV or lounged around chatting with my husband (And BTW, TV is okay as far as blue light goes, so long as you're not sitting with your face up against the screen).
  It's not just the blue-light-emitting devices that are the problem with working before bedtime. It's also that working puts your brain in a stimulated alert mode, when you should be winding down in preparation for sleep. Think of activities you can do to help you with that winding-down process. I know, for me, a hot bath in a candlelit bathroom does the trick.

- *Eliminate interruptions.* Sometimes we can't control those, especially in a house with kids or when we live in a noisy urban neighborhood. But control what you can. Maybe wear earplugs to bed. Turn off your phone so those Facebook notifications don't beep at you. Limit how much water you drink so you don't have to make trips to the bathroom (though it's highly recommended for optimal health to drink a full glass of water before going to sleep).

While we all know people who seem to function at their peak and hardly ever sleep, they aren't you. And they may crash and burn in due time, for all you know.

Take a listen to this bit of testimony an author friend shared with me:

Years ago, when I got serious about finding ways to increase my word count, I decided to track for ninety days all the factors that I thought were interfering with my ability to write: my daily energy level, my mood, how inspired I felt, how much sleep I'd gotten the night before, whether or not I felt sick or was having allergy symptoms, what I ate, whether or not I took vitamins with breakfast.

The results I got were shocking. I'd been sure that I needed to be inspired and in a good mood to write. I'd also been sure that feeling sick was my biggest obstacle. But the data showed that only *one* thing affected whether I was able to write on any given day: how many hours of sleep I'd gotten.

In fact, the amount of sleep correlated with how many words I wrote. Eight to nine hours was a 2,000- to-3,000-word day. Seven to eight produced a 1,000-to-2,000-word day. Six or seven hours meant I'd be lucky to get five hundred words written. Less than six hours of sleep resulted in days where I wrote a sentence, deleted it, and repeated that unproductive loop until my timer went off and the writing session was over.

I wasn't spending more time at the computer on different days either. Those word counts were for three-hour writing sessions. It was almost as if there was a word-count dial in my brain, and how much sleep I got determined what setting that dial was set at.

When I realized that, I stopped using bad moods, sickness, allergic reactions, feeling tired, and everything else as an excuse to skip writing. Tracking allowed me to discover the *real* cause of my unproductive days and to take control of my creative process by doing one simple thing: going to bed early enough to get at least eight hours of sleep.

Wow. I hope you can see how important and helpful it is to take the time to examine your Productivity ABCs, knowing that biology plays a huge part of being productive. And that scrimping on sleep may just be the main reason you aren't super productive.

## One Last Tip

Don't work through your breaks. You need breaks. You may feel you'll be more productive if you give up that half-hour lunch or even a ten-minute "stop and stretch" break, but the opposite is true.

Breaks afford you the opportunity to do some decompressing and reevaluating what you're working on. Breaks give you distance from your project as well as rest your brain. Even if you mentally work through some of your scene, for example, during your break time, being away from your computer and talking a walk can spark new ideas or give you a fresh enthusiasm to jump back in after your break.

Ultimately, you may be a whole lot more productive in the hours after your break than if you worked straight through. And that's why short power naps are also highly recommended by highly productive people.

We're back to the adage: writer, know thyself. Take the time to discover how much sleep you need and what the best times are for you to go to bed and wake up. Make a good night's sleep a priority in your life. For, if you do, it will go a long way toward helping you become a super-productive writer.

*Let's review:*

- *Skipping sleep has detrimental effects on our biology and will, over time, cause us to lose productivity.*

- *When we sleep, our brain clears out toxins.*

- *Aim to develop a natural sleep cycle, and work yourself off drugs to achieve that.*

- *Eliminate caffeine-loaded drinks after noon.*

- *Avoid blue light waves before bedtime.*

- *Aim to wake up around the same time every day, even on days off work.*

- *Stop working before bedtime to fall asleep easier.*

- *Don't let others determine your sleep schedule.*

- *Eliminate interruptions and distractions that might keep you from a sound sleep, whenever possible.*

- *Consider your larger biological cycle and examine if you tend to have more energy, motivation, and focus certain times of the year, then plan your writing accordingly.*

- *Don't work through your breaks. They ultimately help you be more productive.*

# Chapter 6: Diet and Exercise for the Super-Productive Writer

I know. There's nothing more distasteful than talking about diet and exercise. But seriously, how can we weigh in all the biological factors to being productive without discussing this?

I'll try to make this as painless (and guilt-free) as possible.

Stay with me.

Let's take a look first at one of the hard truths about being a writer, and that's the fact we sit to do it. Some writers have learned to write while walking on a treadmill, as I mentioned in an earlier chapter. But I imagine it doesn't work for everyone. That said, let's talk about this briefly.

### Sitting Can Be Bad for Your Health

Writers sit more than they do anything else. We average 9.3 hours a day, compared to 7.7 hours of sleeping. Sitting is so prevalent and so pervasive that we don't even question how much we're doing it. And since writers everywhere are doing it, it doesn't occur to us that it's not great for our health.

Health studies conclude that people should sit less and get up and move around more. The reason is obvious. Our bodies need to move and exercise. While I'm not going to go into the specifics of exercise in this look at productivity, let's just agree that we need it, regularly, to stay healthy and to keep up our energy and concentration.

Each writer has to figure out what the best exercise regime is for his or her own body needs and limitations.

## Here's What Happens When We Sit Too Long

After an hour of sitting, the production of fat-burning enzymes declines by as much as 90%. Extended sitting slows the body's metabolism, and this affects the "good cholesterol" levels in our bodies.

Research shows that the lack of physical activity contributes to heart disease, type 2 diabetes, breast cancer, and colon cancer. The *New York Times* reported on another study, published last year in the journal Circulation, that looked at nine thousand Australians and found that for each additional hour of television a person sat and watched per day, the risk of dying rose by 11%. In that article, a doctor is quoted as saying that excessive sitting, which he defines as nine hours a day, is a lethal activity. Wow, that's me, nearly every day.

Stopping every hour for a few minutes to stretch or power-walk twenty feet to the fridge to get something to eat is not going to counteract this problem.

So I'm not going to go on and on here. I think we all know how bad a sedentary life is for our health. If we want to be super productive, we need to take care of these bodies we have. That means eating healthy foods, getting regular exercise, and taking care of our health in general.

We'll be looking at choices (and habits) next, and the choice to eat right and exercise is one every writer needs to think about. Diet and exercise don't just affect our productivity; they can mean a difference between good and bad health, life and death.

## You Write What You Eat

When we think about the factors that contribute to productivity, we rarely give much consideration to food. For most of us, struggling with overloaded schedules, food is simply fuel.

But the foods we eat affect us greatly. Our cars can function just about the same on different brands of fuel, but our bodies don't act the same way with food.

Food has a direct impact on our cognitive performance, which is why poor choices in what we eat can directly impact our productivity.

The World Health Organization states: "Adequate nutrition can raise your productivity levels by 20 percent on average."

Hit Pause here.

Raise our productivity 20%? That's huge!

Most of us know much of this intuitively, yet we don't always make smart decisions about our diet. In part, it's because we're at our lowest point in both energy and self-control when deciding what to eat. French fries and ice cream are a lot more appetizing when we're mentally drained.

So what are we to do? One thing we most certainly shouldn't do is assume that better information will motivate us to change. We've been talking about motivation a lot, and we all know that it's hard to get motivated to adopt new habits (which we'll be talking about more in upcoming chapters).

Most of us are well aware that scarfing down junk food is not a good life decision. But that doesn't make it any less delicious.

So, as with changing any habits, you first have to decide to change. One thing that will help is to make the conscious decision to alter your eating habits before you get hungry (and don't do your grocery shopping when you're hungry either!).

Another good habit is to have a few well-timed snacks throughout the day (discussed further on) instead of letting your blood sugar get a big spike and then cause an energy meltdown later in the day.

Choose to make it easier to do healthy snacking. In other words, don't buy that junk in the first place. Put healthy snacks in the fridge in a form that's easy to grab (like baby carrots already peeled). Put a container of almonds and some protein bars by your computer.

Contrary to what many of us might assume, the trick to eating right is not learning to resist temptation. It's making healthy eating the easiest possible option. Think about it.

# Glucose and the Brain

Okay, we're going to have a little nutrition lesson here, and if this makes you cringe, I promise to keep it as short and sweet as possible.

Glucose is at the heart of energy. What is glucose?

It's a type of sugar you get from foods you eat, and your body uses it for energy. As it travels through your bloodstream to your cells, it's called blood glucose or blood sugar.

We've all heard something about "blood sugar levels," but you may not have paid much attention to this subject or considered the part it may play in your productivity.

While we are looking at the B in the Productivity ABCs—biology—I would be remiss if I left out a discussion about glucose.

Simply put, we need energy to be productive. We need sugar.

But not just any sugar.

The brain accounts for just 2% of our body weight, but it consumes about 20% of our daily calories (I wonder if we lose weight faster if we concentrate harder). To function well, it needs a constant supply of glucose and fat, and from a healthy source.

Research shows that employees who ate five or more servings of fruit and vegetables at least four times a week were 20% more likely to be productive. (I wonder, though, if that is indicative of an overall healthy lifestyle choice that includes regular exercise, no smoking or excessive alcohol, etc.).

So without spending hours going into all the nuances of diet and nutrition, let's look at how we might eat to be more productive.

What we eat has a direct impact on our productivity. Plain and simple.

When we nourish our brains and bodies with the right foods (at the best times), it positively affects how we think, feel, create, and remember.

So, to sum up: glucose is sugar extracted from the foods we eat, and our brains need glucose. Following so far? Good.

## Not All Foods Are Created Equal

Next point: our bodies don't process all foods at the same rate.

When we eat foods that release glucose quickly (simple sugars), such as soda, candy, pasta, and white bread, we experience a blood sugar spike that gives us a quick energy burst.

But that's followed by a drop in blood sugar that leads to a slump. What happens then? We end up with low energy levels and low productivity. We're likely to stare at the computer screen, our head bobbing, trying to keep our eyes open.

When we eat foods that provide low glycemic carbohydrates, such as found in grains, raw fruits, and raw vegetables, as well as proteins and healthy fats, we provide a steadier supply of energy to the brain.

The way you can get twenty-five grams of glucose into your bloodstream is pretty easy. You can eat a donut, or you can eat a small bowl of oats.

There is little difference in the short term for your brain activity. But over the stretch of a normal eight-hour day, however, the differences are big. After eating a donut, glucose will release into your blood quickly. You'll have an energy burst for about twenty minutes. Then your glucose level will drop like a rock, leaving you unfocused and easy to distract.

The oats, on the other hand, will release their sugar as glucose more slowly. This means you will have a steady glucose level, along with better focus and attention levels.

Another important factor is your leptin level. Leptin signals to your brain how full you are. There's a reason we're often still hungry after we eat junk food. We're not getting the signal that we're full.

## So What Are Some Good Things to Eat?

### Breakfast (or whenever!):

- Eggs contain a fat-like B vitamin called choline that enhances memory and reaction time. Choline increases the size of neurons in the brain, which helps them fire stronger and faster electrical signals.

- Bananas provide about twenty-five grams of glucose, and that's what our brains need circulating in our bloodstream.

- Yogurt (my favorite) has minerals, protein, and probiotics that help with digestion. The water in yogurt helps improve hydration. But don't get yogurt that's packed full of sugar. Consider getting plain yogurt and mixing with fresh fruit and nuts. (I have that for lunch almost daily, and when I eat that, I don't need my afternoon nap!)

- Blueberries are not only full of antioxidants that improve memory, they counteract oxidative stress. Okay, someone actually did a study with rats, giving them blueberries. Results? The rats had greatly improved memory and motor skills, and they experienced a reversal in age-related decline in balance and coordination. (I'm loading up on blueberries!)

## Lunch:

- Since raw fruits and vegetables are the ticket, think about having a salad. I'm a salad addict. I have one nearly every day, year in and year out. I have a lot of energy. I'm sure it has a lot to do with eating salads. Those leafy greens like spinach and kale are so good for you—the minerals and vitamins they contain support the nervous system and improve cognition.

  And there really is a huge difference, both nutritionally and in taste, between homegrown or locally organic veggies and the ones you buy in the big supermarket chain stores. You may not be able to afford a lot of expensive produce, but what's your health worth? Check out local farmers' markets or consider growing some of your own veggies.

- Avocados contribute to healthy blood flow, necessary for a healthy functioning brain.

- Almonds are thought to stimulate the brain and boost your mood and memory. (I crave them, so my body is telling me something. Listen to your body.)

- Virgin (unprocessed) olive oil is so good for you in so many ways, I could write a book about just this one food. Put it in everything you can.

- If you're going to eat bread, make it high in grains and low in sugar. Pair it with protein and butter (or that olive oil).

**Dinner:**

- Salmon is packed with omega 3, protein, iron, and B vitamins, which support memory, recall, reasoning, and focus.

- Brown rice and other whole grains have vitamins and magnesium that improve cognition.

- Broccoli is a superfood with a great source of Vitamin K, which also enhances cognitive function and improves brain power.

- Eggplant will keep your brain sharp by enhancing communication between brain cells and "messenger molecules."

I'm happy to say these are all my favorite foods that I eat more than any others, so I'm assuming they play a big part in my super productivity!

## And Don't Forget the Snacks!

We writers would never get much done if we didn't have snacks! I don't often nibble as I write, but I do take breaks to get a snack during long stretches of writing between meals.

Again, fresh fruits and vegetables are a great choice. Dopamine, found in these foods, plays a key role in motivation and engagement. This is exactly what's needed to be super productive.

I read up on a clinical study done across thirteen days with 405 young adults (67% female, mean age 19.9). The aim of the study was to determine whether eating fruits and vegetables is associated with other markers of well-being beyond happiness and life satisfaction.

Each day, participants reported on their consumption of fruits, vegetables, sweets, and chips, as well as their well-being, curiosity, creativity, positive affect, and negative affect (yes, the study is talking about *affect*, not *effect*).

## Conclusions?

There is growing evidence that a diet rich in fruits and vegetables is related to greater happiness, life satisfaction, and positive affect.

Other recommended snacks are walnuts, cashews, and . . . don't scream . . . wait for it . . . dark chocolate!

I'm not kidding. You have permission to eat chocolate! Run, don't walk, to your stash and grab some right now.

Dark chocolate contains antioxidant properties that increase the production of endorphins (yes, that's why we are so happy when we consume chocolate!) while enhancing focus and concentration.

That's not to say you should binge on chocolate all day long. There's sugar in those pieces. So go for small amounts with low sugar content.

## Let Me Scare You for a Moment

When we eat junk food or high-carb processed foods, it slows down productivity, and it's bad for our health. If you don't believe me, watch the incredible documentary called Super Size Me. It will shake you to your core, and, I hope, you'll never eat another Big Mac again.

Sugary foods, like sodas (a big problem with many people), make you feel weak, confused, nervous, lethargic, and unable to concentrate. They give you that blood sugar crash (and burn).

Heavy calorie-ridden foods, such as burgers and fries, and that side of beer, will make you sleepy and sluggish.

But worse than that, diets dominated by such foods (high in saturated fats) can be damaging to your health. People who eat like this all the time are more susceptible to cognitive deficits and the slow processing of information. They read slower and have trouble remembering.

One study with rats that gorged on saturated fat for weeks suffered brain damage in the hippocampus (poor rats—the blueberry group fared a lot better!), an area critical to memory formation. Eat enough bad fats and you'll forget your name. Not to mention you won't be able to write well or crank out great books.

## Here's Another Interesting Fact about Glucose

In order to make good choices and form good habits, we need strong self-control or willpower. Get this: research suggests that blood glucose is an important source of self-control.

Wow.

Acts of self-control deplete large amounts of glucose. Lack of self-control often occurs when glucose is low or can't be mobilized effectively to the brain. Restoring glucose to a sufficient level typically improves self-control.

Can't get going in your writing? Can't seem to focus and push yourself to write? Maybe you need that chocolate. Or a handful of almonds.

## Don't Skip

Being hungry, or skipping breakfast, can ruin your hours of your productivity. One study had children skipping breakfast before coming to class. Then a random half of the children were given a good breakfast (the others got nothing). Those who ate learned more and misbehaved less. When all the children were given a healthy midmorning snack, though, the differences disappeared.

A portion on a small plate will always fill you up more than the same portion on a large plate.

Weird, huh? If you have trouble controlling how much you eat, give this a try. It could make the difference of one hour of productivity gained each day—just by reducing the size of your plate and being less full.

Instead of consuming three big meals per day, consume five small ones (try to have green vegetables with each meal). You will be much more productive and focused by eating smaller meals so that your digestive system doesn't use most of the energy you have to digest large meals.

We all know what happens if we eat a huge lunch. We end up snoring about an hour later, hunched over the computer.

Keep these tips in mind. Shop for healthy brain-supporting foods and make them more accessible than junk food or high-sugar foods. Have healthy snacks throughout the day, and don't neglect exercise.

## Each of Us Is Different

In addition to regular sleep and scheduling to write to take advantage of your biological prime time, you need to create good eating and exercise habits.

Are you serious about your career as an author? Do you want to write for life?

Then know thyself and work with, not against, your biology.

While researching all this, I learned some neat things. I realized that my body regularly craves almost all the best foods for productivity. I don't think it's just a matter of coincidence that I happen to like these foods. Rather, I believe it's evidence of my body talking to me and I'm listening. In recent years I've come to crave almonds (I also read that they contain something needed during menopause, and that's also a factor in my craving). But I also crave walnuts, avocados, and eggplant.

What I'm thinking is that, while our bodies sometimes scream "Go buy a pizza or a triple-decker ice cream cone," if we strain to listen beyond the superficial craving (which is often our bodies saying "I need glucose"), maybe we can hear that true biological voice telling us what we need as we're cranking out those books.

I'll crave different foods at different times of the year, and I believe that's in line with our biology. Summer is when fruits are plentiful, with their high sugar, to give us lots of energy for heavy outdoor physical activity and hot temperatures. If we consider that we were made to work harder and for more hours in warmer weather, and rest and be mostly dormant during cold seasons, it makes sense. In the winter we long for heavy, thick soups and potatoes. Foods that make us warm and sleepy.

So as you get to know yourself in this biology examination to become a super-productive writer, realize that you are unique, and what works for someone else may not be ideal for you. This is your journey of self-discovery.

## Have Second Thoughts about Eating Late Dinners

Dr. Jamie Koufman, a specialist in the diagnosis and management of acid reflux, noted that over the past two decades, the time of the evening meal has been trending later and later among his patients. He mentioned in an article he wrote that "the after-work meal—already later because of longer work hours—is often further delayed by activities such as shopping and exercise.

"Typical was the restaurateur who came to see me with symptoms of postnasal drip, sinus disease, hoarseness, heartburn, and a chronic cough. He reported that he always left his restaurant at eleven p.m., and after arriving home would eat dinner and then go to bed. There was no medical treatment for this patient, no pills or even surgery to fix his condition. The drugs we are using to treat reflux don't always work, and even when they do, they can have dangerous side effects. My patient's reflux was a lifestyle problem. I told him he had to eat dinner before seven p.m., and not eat at all after work. Within six weeks, his reflux was gone."

His conclusion? "In my experience, the single most important intervention is to eliminate late eating, which in the United States is often combined with portions of large, over-processed fatty food."

For many of us, dinner is the largest meal, and heaviest, of the day. It takes hours for the stomach to empty of food, and as you get older, the process takes longer.

Some medical professionals suggest limiting the hours you take in food to between ten a.m. and seven p.m. This provides what's called "intermittent fasting," which has many benefits, including normalizing your insulin, ghrelin (hunger), and leptin sensitivity; resetting your body to use fat as its primary fuel (instead of carbs); promoting needed HGH (human growth hormone) production; lowering triglyceride levels; and reducing oxidative stress (which can damage cells associated with aging and disease).

Eating late dinners throws off your body's internal clock and leads to weight gain. Mice that were exposed to nighttime light (kept up "past their bedtime") ended up eating more food than normal, but when fed only during daylight hours, they didn't gain weight.

Reread that last sentence.

Do you struggle with your weight?

It could have something to do with eating those big meals right before bedtime.

Studies do show that our bodies are programmed for nocturnal feeding, meaning we might be designed to eat our biggest meal in the evening. Have you ever eaten a huge meal in the middle of the day and felt wiped out? The biological idea of eating in the early evening makes sense. That heavier, bigger meal makes us relaxed and sleepy, aiding us to fall asleep at the right time for our bodies and helping us have a solid night's sleep.

Ideally, give yourself three to four hours between dinner and bedtime. My husband and I have been eating dinner between five and six p.m. pretty much every night since we've been married (aside from date night or special occasions). While not everyone can set a schedule like this, factor these insights into your choices as best you can. It all impacts your overall productivity and health in general.

## One Last Insight about Biology

We've been analyzing our biology as it pertains to daily cycles, but I'd like to talk about seasons and years. Some of us write better at different times of the year. Winter is when I want to nap and hibernate. It's harder for me to push myself in the winter to write, but I've learned to do it. It just might mean I have to stop and take a nap on any given day, or cut short my writing time.

If you're aware that your body has different needs at different times of the year, respect that. If you have a lot more energy and motivation in the summer, try to make time to write more during those months.

I rarely write every day. Well, I do write something every day. But when it comes to my books, I may go months between writing. Since I do my best when I write for long hours day after day in a kind of marathon (that's something I've learned about myself), I often schedule a block of weeks to write a novel from start to finish. This isn't just about biology but schedule.

Summer is when I like to hike and backpack. I want to be outdoors. I will tell my editing clients I'm taking time off, and I'll cut way back on my work schedule.

All that fresh air and beautiful scenery inspires me to write. So it's not surprising that many of my novels have been cranked out between August 1 and October 1. I usually set aside all of December to write as well. My editing load is usually light then, due to the holidays. So why not write?

So think about this bigger picture and spend time doing some strategic planning that keeps in mind your biology. Use my ebook Strategic Planning for Writers—4 Easy Steps to Success, which you get for free when you join my mailing list (or, if you're already on my list and didn't get it, let me know and I'll send you a copy).

My book will help you strategize milestones and doable goals for your career in one-, two-, and five-year chunks. But be sure to lay out those goals with your biology in mind! You'll be way more productive if you do.

*Let's review:*

- *Sitting too many hours every day is bad for our health. We need to move around and get regular exercise.*

- *The foods we eat greatly impact our ability to concentrate, get motivated, and be productive, so we need to be mindful and knowledgeable about our diet.*

- *We need to make healthy foods easily accessible so we won't have to work hard to choose them over junk food.*

- *Our brains need a lot of calories, and providing a good source of glucose will do much to help us be super productive.*

- *Our bodies don't process all foods at the same rate, and we want to avoid quick sugar rushes that raise our glucose level, then drop it suddenly.*

- *Diets rich in raw fruits and vegetables can improve our happiness and outlook, which impacts our motivation and productivity.*

- *Our willpower or self-control (sit in the chair and write!) is affected by our glucose levels.*

- *Skipping meals and being hungry can negatively impact our productivity.*

- *Try to avoid eating late dinners, giving yourself three to four hours between dinner and bedtime.*

- *Your diet needs may vary at different times of the year. Learn to listen to your body.*

# Chapter 7: Distractions and Retraining Your Brain

Ah, distraction. The bane of our modern existence. Face it—we are going to be deluged with distractions every waking moment of the day. Unless you've found a way to live in a bubble or at the top of a mountain, deep in a cave, you probably are going to have some distractions. Even then, that water dripping from the ceiling in a steady rhythm is going to start distracting you.

I think the problem is worse than we know. Because decades ago, we just didn't have the kinds of distractions we have now. And because we are now so used to being connected online to everyone else in the world (or so it seems) around the clock, it's more a problem of our habits than anything else.

So now we're going to go deep into the "C" of our Productivity ABCs: our choices, which impact our behavior. And retraining our brain is a choice writers need to make if they're to be super productive.

## How We've Ruined Our Brain

For instance, my brain is now so used to derailing at any given second, even when I'm backpacking alone in the Sierras, away from any cell phone signals, it takes me days to decompress and allow my brain to settle into what feels like a natural state of being and observation. I have to confess I now take my phone and solar charger with me so I can read and play games and listen to music on my phone while out in the wilderness. But I'm thinking of making a resolution to leave the tech back in civilization. Because it's starting to control me and not the other way around.

And I'm not the worst offender—not by far. I look at a lot of young people when I'm out about town. Even in the movie theater, they're texting on their phone. I went to an NBA game recently (and those tickets aren't cheap), and the couple in front of us never got off their phones. They never watched the game. They took selfies one after the other, then texted them to their friends. I know all this because the section we sat in was steep, and we looked down right into their phones.

We moved to some other seats; I just couldn't take it after a half hour. Later, at halftime, I saw the couple on the concourse. *Good*, I thought, *they're taking a tech break.* But no. They were standing near the wall, charging their phones so they could keep up the texting for the second half of the game.

I really wanted to scream. Sometimes I think smartphones are the worst thing that's ever happened to us. Computers? Great. But once phones added on texting and email and cameras, that was the beginning of the end.

Yes, I'm a hypocrite, because I use it all. And I know I'm way too dependent on my phone. But I'm thinking of putting some limitations on—for my sanity.

Have you ever forgotten your phone for the day? Left it at home by accident? Be honest—did you nearly (or truly) fall apart? What if you chose one day a week to be without tech? Or at least without your phone?

I wonder how many of us could get through the day.

## The Curse of Our Era

I say all this because what's at the heart of the problem is the *habit* we've developed. Back in the age of the dinosaurs (my childhood), each household had one phone number and usually a few big old phones hardwired into the wall. You've seen it in the movies or old TV shows—that thing with the dial? And the super long stretchy cord that allowed you to get away from Mom, who was in the kitchen preparing dinner, so you could talk to your girlfriend or boyfriend.

Some parents limited the time their teens could talk on the phone. I would sneak the phone into my room late at night to talk to my boyfriend. Good thing it was a local number. Long-distance calls were not only expensive, they showed up on the phone bill.

Cell phones and mobile phones were nonexistent until my daughters were in their late teens. So even up until then, phones were rarely used. You told your kids to "call when you get there and call when you're leaving." That was about it for phone use. Kids and adults actually spent time together, and just about the only time they communicated was when in person, face-to-face. Imagine that.

I know I'm wandering down memory lane, but, in some ways, I'm nostalgic for that quieter, simpler, less distracting time. We moved slower, paid more attention. We lived in the "now" moment and actually experienced life.

I can honestly say I believe few people in our culture today do any of that. I know people who are so busy snapping pictures every second that they actually aren't experiencing the life they are documenting. They spend hours looking at their photos, ones they took that day. But they actually, to me, weren't "there."

So what's the point of saying all this?

## Multitasking Is Great, Right?

All this tech has helped us to multitask, and that's great, right?

Wrong. We've ruined our brains. What we do each day, every second of the day, is not natural. It's not healthy. We may feel we are super productive, and we may be multitasking with the best of them. But here are some interesting statistics that studies have presented:

- Multitaskers experience a 40% drop in productivity.

- Multitaskers take 50% longer to accomplish a single task than if focusing only on that task.

- Multitaskers make up to 50% more errors.

- It takes four times longer to recognize new things when we multitask.

- Up to 40% more time is needed to switch tasks.

- Multitasking costs the US economy $650 billion a year in lost productivity.

- 31 workweeks are lost each year due to multitasking.

When we jump from task to task or from one activity to another at such regular and alarming rates (I tend to check my email every couple of minutes, on my bad days, and that's exacerbated if I'm working on something I'm not all that into), we don't get into our groove. We don't find our flow.

To be a productive writer, you gotta get into that zone. And stay there for a while.

Our writing suffers when we let ourselves get distracted. And while I'll get into habits and distraction in more depth, I want to first talk about how we can retrain (and restrain) our brains, now that we've ruined them. (Maybe I should make T-shirts that say "Reclaim Your Brain—Unplug.")

How do you know if you need to retrain your brain?

If tasks that should take thirty minutes take you an hour to complete, or if you constantly find yourself wander the halls of the Internet on your phone or other device, checking social media sites and texting a friend, the answer is yes.

Larry Rosen, PhD, a research psychologist and author of *Disorder: Understanding Our Obsession with Technology and Overcoming Its Hold on Us* says we rarely focus on and attend to any task for more than three to five minutes without getting distracted.

"The bottom line is we are all constantly self-distracting, whether you're in school, at your job, or just at home."

His advice? We have to retrain our brain to respond based on a set schedule rather than spontaneous cues (such as beeps and bells and pop-ups telling us someone or some app is sending us a message).

# How to Retrain Your Brain

Easiest way to do this is to turn everything off.

If you're working on your computer, close all windows but the one you're working in. I keep open my Word doc and my Dictionary program. Turn off notifications on your computer. Turn off your phone or stick it under your pillow in your bedroom. Then shut the bedroom door.

This makes me think of my favorite Frog and Toad story. Toad made cookies, then took them to Frog's house. They're so good, they can't stop eating them. Frog puts the cookies in the box, but Toad says, "We can just open the box." Then Frog ties string around the box. Toad then says, "We can just untie the string." You get the drift. Even when the box is tied and placed on a high shelf, they know they can just get the ladder and take them down. The solution?

Frog takes the box outside and scatters the cookies for the birds to eat.

"Now we have no more cookies to eat," said Toad sadly. "Not even one."

"Yes," said Frog, "but we have lots and lots of willpower."

"You may keep it all, Frog," said Toad. "I am going home to bake a cake."

Are you lacking willpower? We're ruined our brains in that regard as well. We hear something and we have to run, not walk, to Facebook and post about it. It may not serve you best to throw your tech out for the birds to eat (or the deer to trample). But you have to start somewhere to retrain your brain.

Here's what Rosen suggests:

Start small. Set an alarm for one minute. During that minute, you can check your email, jump on Twitter, whatever. When that minute is up, stop.

Then set your alarm for fifteen minutes—the average person's maximum attention span in this modern age. Now you have to work for those fifteen minutes—hunker down and write—without your attention wandering. You can do that, can't you?

Repeat.

Don't just put your phone facedown on the desk during your writing time. Make sure all distractions are eliminated so you don't see them. If something pops up (those are deadly!) to notify you of something, it's going to make your switch your focus and get out of your writing zone.

In the evening, I hear continual *dings* on my phone, telling me there are four minutes left in the game, and the Spurs are up three points over the Raptors. Since there are sometimes eight games going on in an evening, you can imagine how many alarms sound—on both my phone and my husband's. But hey, that's okay, because we're watching a game or three at that time. There's a time to allow notifications and a time to shut them off.

Once you are comfortable with fifteen minutes of distraction-free work time, which may take anywhere from a few days to a couple of weeks, bump it up to twenty, then twenty-five, then thirty minutes. "Once you are at thirty minutes, that works," Rosen says.

## Let Others Know You're in Brain Retraining

Need help and accountability? Tell family and friends you are doing this and to not interrupt you during writing time. While you can't control every single bit of your environment or avoid emergencies, you can create this new habit in order to retrain your brain.

During that one minute in which you can check your email, if you have a pressing situation that is going to take longer, write the person and tell him, "I'm in the middle of writing and will get back to you at one p.m." That way you can get that worry off your brain and get back to writing without distraction.

If someone takes offense, just tell them the truth. That you are trying to retrain your brain to focus and not give in to distractions.

Some companies are scheduling in "phone-checking" time during a long meeting for this very purpose. They want their employees to pay attention to the meeting but know if they don't give them breaks to deal with their "stuff," they may lose concentration and be distracted.

We've programmed our brains to believe that if we don't stop what we're doing and check the world out there, we'll miss out on something important. The Internet has brought the entire world into our private lives, and something important and impacting is always going on in the world every second. We can't keep up.

## No, We Don't Have To

Thing is, we believe we have to. Until we can reprogram our brains to believe we *don't* have to be up on everything at any given moment, we will be at the mercy of our tech. Instead of making tech work for us.

"If [tech] is driving you, then you need to become the driver again," Rosen says.

That's a whole lot harder to do than it sounds. But by trying this method Rosen suggests, it may be the first step toward untying the umbilical cord.

Seriously, if you want to become a super-productive writer, you're going to have to learn how to do this to some extent. Keep in mind those statistics about multitasking. It's a productivity killer. You're just going to have to bite the bullet and change some of your habits.

Yes, life was simpler back in the day before all this tech. We lived at a slower pace. But in many ways, we got a whole lot more done—because we didn't have the distraction, and our brains weren't ruined. I, for one, am all for working my way back to a less distracting daily routine. How about you?

*Let's review:*

- *Our technological lifestyle has ruined our brain, so we must find ways to get our brains on track.*

- *We tend to be easily distracted, so we have to find ways to lock out those distractions.*

- *We may feel we're being productive when we multitask, but we're actually not.*

- *Examine yourself to see if you are "self-distracting."*

- *Retrain your brain by developing and adopting a schedule to focus on just your writing.*

- *Turn off distractions when writing.*

- *Set a timer to write without distraction, training yourself to focus unhindered for longer and longer stretches of time.*

- *We need to teach our brains to believe we don't need to pay attention to every distraction.*

- *We need to be the driver, not the driven, when it comes to tech.*

- *It may be hard, but to be super productive, we will have to change some habits!*

# Chapter 8: Hacking Your Way to Productivity

Today, the word *hack* has taken on a different meaning than what it used to mean. Previously, when you hacked into something, it usually involved an ax or sledgehammer. Something that would cause some serious damage.

We've also heard about people who hack or break into computer systems.

But there's a different kind of hacking that's helpful to writers, and in this case *hacking* means a workaround. Finding a back door to slip in through. This is all about habits and our choices. If we can find workarounds that work for us, we can turn them into habits—by choice—and fast track to productivity.

When it comes to our brains, it helps at times to do a little hacking. We can be our own worst enemy when it comes to being productive. Bear with me on this. I'll explain.

We make a lot of excuses when it comes to our writing. We trip ourselves up with our insecurities and fear of rejection or failure. We might try to give ourselves a pep talk, but that usually doesn't work. Because it's never worked before.

Even if our critique group loves our book, we won't believe it. Even if I tell a writer his novel is great and almost ready to be published—the writer will freeze up, procrastinate, find ways to not finish his novel.

This goes into self-sabotage, which, I promise, I'll be discussing at length further along.

But right now I want to talk about productivity hacks. These are choices we make to push past the roadblocks we ourselves set in our path. We're looking at the "C" in our Productivity ABCs, and that's choices. Choosing how to handle these roadblocks can make the difference between our being a static writer and a super-productive one.

**Productive People Create Hacks That Work for Them**

Inc.com has a great slide show featuring thirteen CEOs and their work hacks. Here are a few, to get your brain simmering:

Bryan Guido Hassin, a university professor and start-up junkie, uses "Airplane Days." After noticing that he got some of his best work done on long intercontinental flights, Guido established "Airplane Days" to help him get things done. On "Airplane Days," Guido restricts his Internet access, removes distractions, and churns through his high priority to-do items. He says:

> At the beginning of each week, I carefully look at my schedule and declare one day (or two half days) to be Airplane Time. I block it out on my shared calendar and treat it as if I were in the air: working out of the office, disabling my phone, and shutting off network connections on my laptop. The rest of the days are for meetings, etc., but this blocked-out time each week is my most productive by far.

Is he really on a plane? No. But he's pretending he is. This is his hack to get around his usual succumbing to distractions.

Alok Bhardwaj, the founder of Hidden Reflex, a software start-up, says he starts his day by doing the least desirable task first. He recommends starting your day this way:

1. Do least desirable tasks first thing in the morning. Try to work two to three hours straight on getting stuff done first thing in thing in the morning, before email or anything else.

2. Do not read any news or anything similar while working.

3. Use your workspace for work only.

4. Go through a daily to-do list of three to five things you *must* get done.

5. Don't try to do too much, don't try to optimize too much, delegate, stay focused on the big picture.

6. Exercise, meditate every day.

Here's a variation on Rosen's suggestion (discussed in the previous chapter):

Christian Sutardi, a cofounder at Lolabox, uses David Allen's famous "Two-Minute Rule." Sutardi explains: "For two months now I've been following David Allen's famous 'Two-Minute Rule.' It's very simple: when a new task comes in and I see that I can do it in less than two minutes, then I do it right away. This easy rule increased my productivity a lot. I love it, because it's not a groundbreaking rule, it's no fancy app or software, it doesn't even require learning or dedication, and you can start doing it today."

Jason Kanigan, a sales trainer, says, "Figure out when your 'golden hours' are, and protect them at all costs. Permit no distractions during those times. Then 'Eat That Frog'— pick the biggest, hairiest, most difficult goal that stands between you and the next giant step toward success . . . and do it now. A small number of decisions make up the majority of your life experience. Therefore, a small number of activity choices make up the large majority of your achievements . . . or lack thereof."

Are you starting to get some ideas of how you might hack your way to productivity? It's not just the scheduling that might need hacking. It's also your mind-set.

We looked at the need to change the way we talk to ourselves, to be positive in our thinking. That's a hack to productivity.

So how do we ensure we're as productive as we can be?

By being courageous.

## Boldly Go . . .

Some writers lack courage because they aren't distinguishing between real and perceived risk.

We're afraid of failure, so instead of focusing on the one project staring us in the face, we split our attention among various projects. We tend to go with what's safe, what's worked before.

Becoming a super-productive writer means venturing out into some uncharted territory for us. We are setting aside huge blocks of time on a chance. We may be spending valuable time that we feel should be spent making reliable money so we can support ourselves or our families. It's easy to make excuses because they're good excuses.

So by procrastinating and spreading our attention widely, we guarantee that none get the time and energy each deserves. A book is a demanding mistress, and she does demand a lot of time and energy. Anyone who's written a full-length book can attest to this.

We may feel if we use a lot of book hacks (quick learning aids) to plow our way through our project, we'll do justice to it. But we won't. When it comes to mastering the skills to write a book, you just can't hack that.

So hack what you can. Use mental and emotional hacks to find a back door to being super productive.

We all have roughly the same access to the tools we need to be productive, but it's the courage to push through (hack through) our resistance that separates the doers and the wishers.

It's said that we only have two to four hours of high-level energy per day. (I have a whole lot more than that, but it's taken years of discipline and cementing habits to get there.) Those two to four hours translate to about ten to twenty hours a week. A lot of writers can be super productive putting in only ten hours of writing a week. (I've written full-length novels in three months on just that number of hours.)

Once we use up those peak hours, we hit a wall. We still might have energy to do other things that are important, but we aren't at our peak performance.

So pushing through to try to do more can sometimes stress us unnecessarily. Just as with determining your peak times to work, you don't want to lay a guilt trip on yourself if you aren't able to get more done.

This is why I'm against setting a word-count requirement. Some days we write slower. Some scenes are harder to write. When we demand a word count for the day before we stop writing (many successful writers do this), we put a lot of undue pressure (maybe we should change it to "undo" pressure, since it ends up unraveling us) on ourselves. Especially if we don't have the luxury to write all day and night and quit when we finally hit that mark.

So instead of working longer or harder, we should work smarter. Creating those hacks will help. But they aren't the solution to being a terrific writer. You still have to put into practice what you learn.

### How about Some Little Hacks?

*Aim for In-box Zero is a good objective.* If we know we have a pile-up of emails we need to get to, it can prey on our minds when we're trying to focus on our writing. By creating numerous personal folders in our mail program, we have a place to put them all.

Create one folder labeled "to do today."

When you take that one minute to glance through your emails (after every half hour of writing, if that's the schedule you've decided upon), see which emails can first be deleted, which ones can be answered in that one minute (sometimes a "hey, thanks!" is all you need to respond with) and then answer those, and then assess which ones need to be answered but will take more than a minute. Stick those in your "to do today" folder.

When you've finished putting in those hours of writing, you know where to find them. Sometimes by setting something on a shelf, knowing it's there and waiting for us, we can then forget about it and get our work done.

To-do lists are great for that. So long as I have my to-do list at hand, if a thought pops into my head (which it often does) while I'm writing (whether it's something I have to do or a cool idea for my next novel), I can jot it down quickly and forget about it until later. I "reward" myself after getting my writing done by indulging in replying to my emails. Sure, it's something I need to do, but now, when my brain is tired and not at its peak (as we looked at earlier), answering emails is just the thing. I get a nice sense of completion at the end of the day when the writing is finished and my emails have been moved out of my in-box, and my "to do today" box is empty.

You may need a folder called "to do this month." Some things will take time, or aren't top priorities and so can be put off awhile. But clearing them out of your in-box helps avoid distraction.

*Write things down right away that come to mind.* As mentioned above, a great hack is to carry around a notepad or even your smartphone if it has a notes program. I'm always stopping to jot down a note about a word or idea to use in my novel. If I'm driving, I tell my phone to take a note, and then I dictate the note so it's written down for me. Later I'll move those bits into my big notebooks that I use for reference when writing my books. Think about using a to-do-list app like Wunderlist, if you need something organized and simple.

*Schedule "stressing" time.* Here's a great hack if you tend to let things build in the back of your mind that stress you. They could be world issues or family problems. Whatever they are, set a time during the day (best to make this either before or after you get that chunk of writing done) to dive into your stress. Say, twenty minutes to go all-in, even talking to yourself or kicking a tree or something while you're on a roll. But when that time is up, you're done. You've dealt with the stress and now can at least put it aside for a while, so you can be productive in your writing. This is a workaround, not a cure-all.

*Choose some uplifting surfing time.* If you need a break and want to get on social media, instead of jumping into the usual, try exploring some different topic or site you don't usually visit. Maybe look for recipes on Pinterest. Or find a hash tag on Twitter that points to your favorite movie and see what people are saying about it. Better yet, go to an astronomy site or other science site that can teach you cool facts about the universe and show you beautiful pictures of galaxies. Learning a few new, intriguing facts that you can share with others is refreshing.

*Limit your daily to-do list to just five key items.* Sure, you have a heck of a lot more you need to get done each day. Some are so routine (put up the laundry, prep meals, etc.) you don't really have to put them on your list. But think about some specific tasks you'd really like to complete today. It could be "go through my shirt drawer and organize" or "write one scene in my novel."

Every day is different and has its own challenges and demands. Some days you can get a whole lot more done than other days. But if you put lots of tasks on your list each day and hardly get most of them even halfway done, it can lead to perpetual frustration and being unduly hard on yourself.

This goes back to that attitude adjustment and the positive way of talking to yourself. But since it's hard for many of us to suddenly change the inner dialogue (easier to change our characters' dialogue than our own), engaging in small hacks can push our attitude along the right track. And the best hacks are those that help us *change* our habits—which we'll get into next.

*Let's review:*

- *Sometimes we have to come up with hacks to get around our attitudes.*

- *Hacks "psych us out" so we can be super productive.*

- *Fear of failure can stymie us, so we need to hack around that fear.*

- *Don't just work harder; work smarter.*

- *Aim for "In-box Zero," and set specific times to check your email.*

- *Write things down right away, then forget them so you can get back to writing.*

- *Schedule some "stressing" time, if needed.*

- *Schedule uplifting "surfing" time.*

- *Simplify your daily to-do list so it's not eating at you or distracting you.*

- *Take time to think of hacks that will get you around yourself so you can write.*

# Chapter 9: Getting a Handle on Habits

We all have bad or counterproductive habits, and sometimes we make excuses for them. "I just can't stop ___" (Fill in the blank with your standby excuse). Well, if some of your habits are getting in the way of being a super-productive writer, then maybe you will have to do away with them.

And the easiest way to do so is to replace them with some new habits. This falls under the C of our Productivity ABCs: choices. Because, whether we like to admit it or not, habits are choices. While research shows that it takes about sixty-six days for a habit to fully form, who knows how long it takes to *break* a long and deeply entrenched one? Yes, habits may be hard to break, but we can choose to either continue them, change them, or eliminate them. Our choice.

So let's take a look at ways we can get into the habit of writing.

Have trouble getting into writing? Do you sit and stare at your computer screen even when you've done your homework and have your scene plotted out?

### Take a Half Hour to Journal

Think about starting your day or preparing your launch into writing by journaling.

While you're sitting having that cup of green tea (instead of that coffee?), think about doing a little writing by hand in a blank journal. Or a journal that has writing prompts. You could write about anything that comes into your head, whether it has to do with you or not.

According to a study done by the Harvard Business School, journaling is one of the best ways to improve professional performance. Occasionally writing by hand improves both memory and creativity, so consider journaling the old-fashioned way: with pen and paper.

Elizabeth George, my favorite mystery writer, speaks about this in her terrific book *Write Away*. She shares excerpts of her daily musings in her chapters.

Writing like this is akin to turning on a faucet to an unused water source. Rusty water comes sputtering out for a while, but soon the water runs smooth and clear.

Sometimes we need this kind of jumpstarting to get our creative juices flowing.

If you have something pressing on your mind, maybe some personal issues you're dealing with, and you feel they might invade your writing time, take a half hour and journal about them. This is another of those hacks to help you get past yourself to be productive.

If the habit of trying to psyche yourself into writing doesn't work, change the habit. Unplug, get away from the Internet and those pop-up notifications, and sit somewhere quiet and peaceful. Gush out all those things on your mind, lock them in your pages, then close the book and head to your computer to get the day's writing done.

## Let Your Characters Run Amok

If you want to align yourself with your day's project, you can come up with a fun prompt the ties in with your novel. Try freewriting in your POV character's voice. Put her in the setting of your upcoming scene. Throw in some other characters or even some crazy aardvark that talks with a bad English accent. Let yourself go with the creativity.

This is a great way to give room for your brain to explore your characters and let them come to life. You may discover intriguing aspects of their personality or secrets they reveal to you that stun you. Details you can use in a big way in your novel.

I truly believe once you create characters and give them the space to come to life, they do and they will. Many authors will tell you how their characters have run amok and taken over the stage, going off script. While that can be a bad thing for your plot (you do have to remember who's in charge here), giving them license to come alive helps you create highly memorable characters.

So, think about spending a half hour before you dig into your scene writing and noodle on the page. You may want to do this on your computer, but I'd like to encourage you to first try pen and paper. First off, for most people, having to write by hand makes them slow down. And because it's a very different body experience than typing (and you can do this sitting outside or while taking a bath or in positions you might not easily manage when seated at a computer), it engages your brain in a fresh way.

**Try Psyching Yourself Out by Working in Another Document**

When I'm worried about a scene I'm preparing to write (because it's challenging, even daunting), I'll open up a new Word doc and dive into writing the scene there. It's a mental hack that works for me and gets the roadblock out of the way.

I tell myself this is a throwaway document. I don't want to "contaminate" my novel's "keeper" manuscript with something experimental or that might suck in a big way.

What happens when I write a lone scene in a blank document is I unburden myself of the pressure to "perform."

Seriously, this works amazingly. Just knowing I can toss out this document (yes, I know I could also just cut out the scene from the main manuscript as well, but it feels more like failure when I do that) frees me up. In fact, I've written my best "keeper" scenes this way. And when I copy and paste the finished scene into my novel, I feel super productive!

If your manuscript is staring at you in challenge, and you feel like you've lost before you've even written the first line of a scene, try this hack and see if it works for you.

# How to Gain Control over Your Writing

Let's say you've gotten into your scene you're writing and you're suddenly feeling stressed. Pressures are building because those little issues you've been struggling with in your life are sneaking into your brain. Maybe, because of this, your scene is starting to suck.

Don't panic or give up for the day. Maybe that's been your habit. An easy out. Procrastination. "I'll do better tomorrow, once I take care of X, Y, and Z." While that's sometimes the truth, too many writers put off for tomorrow day after day, and we all know there is no tomorrow. There is only today.

So when your writing time turns sour, *step away from your computer.* Get up and take a walk, clear your head. Play ball with your dog. Bake some cookies. But give yourself just a half hour (set an alarm), then go sit back down.

If you just can't get into that scene, *set it aside*. Work on a different scene. Plot another section of your novel. Read through some earlier chapters to hear how they sound. Write your back cover copy that you'll need when it's time to publish. All of this is part of being productive.

Some days I'm just a crappy writer. I can't come up with fresh words or delightful turns of phrases. I'm just writing junk. That's when I switch to these other tasks as part of my writing time.

Don't let that negative, condemning thinking slip in. Don't be hard on yourself if you can't write that great scene and you end up throwing out the last two hours' worth of work. Know this is all part of the wonderful life of an author. Enjoy the ride.

That positive attitude we talked about at the outset is essential. If it's your habit to talk down at yourself, change that habit. Replace the negative with the positive, as I discussed earlier.

So anytime you are writing and you hit a wall, get up, move around, do something else for a half hour, then sit down and try again. If it's just not happening, choose some other related tasks to complete so you have a productive day.

Some days all I do is research. Since I write historical novels set in the West in the 1870s, I have to do a ton of homework. I have dozens of books I study and highlight, and I have a notebook of more than a hundred pages of terms, sayings, descriptions of clothing and vehicles and guns, and historical events details. When I can't get far along in my writing, I study and take notes. And usually that sparks great plot and scene ideas. Which gets my juices flowing again so that my fingers often jump back onto my laptop keyboard and start writing away. That's one way I hack into productivity.

## Maybe You're Overcommitting to Writing

Sometimes we push ourselves too hard. I mentioned earlier how we only have so many highly productive hours in a day, and we each need to determine where those fall on the clock. If we work many more hours during times when we're not at our peak or should be winding down for sleep, we can lose productivity.

I see this often with writers who set a daily word count (which, I believe, for many is a bad idea). They'll push to get that word count if it kills them. Well, it usually doesn't kill them, but it might add a whole lot of unnecessary stress, make them grumpy and snap at their family members, and drain their creativity so what they do write is lousy.

While I set loose goals for my writing (get one scene done a day, for example), I don't set these in concrete. If I've got a rush editing job, I'll forego the writing for that day. Maybe if I finish that job a day earlier than expected, I'll reward myself with a full day of writing (with chocolate trimmings).

If your writing time is limited and often interrupted by things you can't control or ignore, you'd do better to undercommit to your writing. While you may be able to get those around you to leave you alone for one hour while you hide in your office and write, you may feel, then, that "the pressure's on" and you have to hurry to get that scene or chapter written.

Most people don't work well under that type of time pressure. Even though I like tough deadlines, which push me to be super productive, most people are not like me. Research shows that for most, tough self-imposed deadlines don't work. And some who say they like deadlines and are more productive are just, in actuality, more stressed or neurotic.

## Use Your Weird Time to Your Advantage

Weird time, according to Naomi Dunford, marketer, consists of those little snatches of time that land in your lap when you're waiting somewhere for something. You might be in line at the library, sitting in your car waiting for the kids to come out the school's double doors, or in the dentist office waiting to be called in.

Most of us just play games on our phone or text someone (or if you're like that couple at the game, you take selfies repeatedly).

Maybe all that weird time adds up to a half hour. Maybe more.

Could you use that time to write? If not actually write a scene, how about toying with scene ideas? Character quirks? Coming up with names for characters and places?

I'm not suggesting you get obsessive and put every "free" second of your life to work, but instead of getting frustrated while waiting, or "killing time" (violent expression, isn't it?) by playing Solitaire on your phone, why not be productive and work through a plot problem that's been bugging you?

If you feel as if you've lost control over your writing and writing life, this may be a helpful hack to get you back in the saddle. Yeehaw!

## Turn Mundane into Productive

In addition to *weird* time there's *mundane* time. We all have plenty of that. Washing dishes, folding laundry, even jogging on the treadmill.

No way I'm going to get through my half hour on the treadmill five times a week if I don't have my phone on. I listen to podcasts (writing shows, uplifting sermons, gospel music). Sometimes I watch TV episodes—lately I'm going through all the seasons, again, of *Merlin*.

I mentioned that I'm playing with the idea of getting a work station I can set up on my treadmill so I can walk while I write. It's appealing to me, especially because I hate sitting still and get stiff and sore at my computer all day long.

Okay, your hands are often occupied while you're engaged in mundane activities. Doesn't mean you can't listen to or watch something inspiring or instructive. Something that might tie in with your WIP. I like listening to author interviews, to get tips on writing or hear what helpful writing habits an author might have (such as writing while walking on a treadmill . . .).

How about writing workshops or seminars that you bought or downloaded but haven't listened to? Think about subscribing to podcasts such as Michael Hyatt's *This Is Your Life* or Joanna Penn's *The Creative Penn Podcast*.

These are more useful habits you can form that will help you become a super-productive writer.

And is it possible that you could afford to hire an assistant (maybe a virtual one) part-time to do some of the tasks you feel are mundane or tedious and you don't want to do? I hire assistants all the time. I don't spend all that much money on them, in light of the payoff for me.

Presently I have a friend who does a bunch of Pinterest work for me (since I don't know and don't care to learn how that all works). I have an assistant that puts in about ten hours a month helping me with marketing and writing newsletter blasts. He does a lot of little techy things that intimidate and aggravate me. For example, I really don't want to understand how to create a zap on Zapier to connect my online school to my targeted Mailchimp list. It's worth it to me to pay him so I don't get stressed. I've even paid a friend on occasion to post images on Instagram or send out queries to book reviewers. If I have a lot of these tedious things on my to-do list and I don't delegate, I'll get burned out or overly stressed, especially if I really want them to get done.

## Routine Leads to Efficiency

Now that you know your peak productivity hours and how many hours of sleep you need, aside from those commitments on your schedule that you can't change (such as when the kids need to be dropped off and picked up from school), the more you can turn habits into daily or weekly routines (done at the same time each day), the better off you'll be.

First off, having a schedule for doing many tasks takes out the confusion and the wasted time spent trying to fit things in at odd or inconvenient times.

Nobel Prize–winning author Toni Morrison said this in an interview:

> I, at first, thought I didn't have a ritual, but then I remembered that I always get up and make a cup of coffee while it is still dark—it must be dark—and then I drink the coffee and watch the light come. . . . I realized that for me this ritual comprises my preparation to enter a space that I can only call nonsecular. . . . Writers all devise ways to approach that place where they expect to make the contact, where they become the conduit, or where they engage in this mysterious process.
>
> I tell my students one of the most important things they need to know is when they are at their best, creatively. They need to ask themselves, What does the ideal room look like? Is there music? Is there silence? Is there chaos outside or is there serenity outside? What do I need in order to release my imagination?

And again, if you "know thyself," you know what's going to work best for you.

In the survey I sent out to super-productive writers, I found it interesting that the "one bit of advice" they would give to aspiring authors all had to do with routine. Note some of their comments:

"Know what you're going to do before you sit down. Even if it's just a one-sentence description of the scene you plan to write."

"Schedule writing time, even if it's just short slots—e.g., half an hour. Hold yourself accountable to someone—a writing buddy, your Facebook followers, your online writing group."

"Decide you want to write. And then DO it no matter what—just as you would make your bed and brush your teeth everyday!"

"Write every day."

And 100% agreed with this statement (the only statement they all agreed with): "To be super productive, you need to plan your projects and allocate your time carefully, then stick to the plan."

Here's one way I "know myself." I just cannot get into my writing zone in the morning until I've cleared my in-box. Sorry, not happening. I won't focus if I keep wondering who's emailed me. An editing client might be asking me a question, and I don't like to put clients off. Or a friend wants some help with something.

If I get through my in-box (which can be fifty-plus emails), I feel ready to face the day without distraction. No, I don't eat in the morning, because I'm not a breakfast person. But you might be. If you need to eat a meal or even a piece of toast before writing, then eat.

You've probably already got a routine for many of your habits. But one way to check if some are falling through the cracks is to jot down everything you do during the day. Do this for a week or two. Just a quickie "checked my email 8:10-8:30" or "washed the dishes 10:15-10:30."

Here's a hack I do with routine. I hate folding large piles of laundry. So I'll dump the clean, dry pile on my bed or leave it in the basket by my worktable. Then, every time I pass the pile, I fold three items. That's all. Instead of taking fifteen minutes to fold it all, to me it's as if I'm not really doing any laundry at all, ever.

Okay, laugh. I'm rolling my eyes. I know. Dumb. But it's just a habit I've gotten into. Somehow, while I'm getting those scenes written, my laundry gets folded. Voila! Magic! If Astro is lying in the basket, on top of all the laundry, it may take longer to get it done. I just don't have the heart to kick the kitty off the pile.

Spending hours on social media, are we? How about you schedule two fifteen-minute blocks around your peak writing time for that? Go ahead and set that timer, if you tend toward addiction and obsession. I allow myself about ten minutes to check the news apps on my phone in the morning as well. If you have to, get one of those apps that prevents you from going online for set periods of time.

My survey respondents listed the overuse of the Internet as the #1 habit they needed to eliminate. Clearly they must have gotten that habit under control since they crank out multiple books a year.

Don't get all crazy about this. The idea here is to create some good habits *via routine* so that you streamline your time. Too many people waste way too much time, and part of that time is spent complaining how unproductive they are and can't seem to ever get any writing done. I'm just trying to help you look at your habits so you can be that super-productive writer you dream of being.

It's as easy as ABC: attitude, biology, and choices.

*Let's review:*

- *We all know our habits, and we know which ones are getting in the way of our writing. We need to be determined to change some habits.*

- *Journaling before writing can get the creative juices flowing and unblock resistance to writing.*

- *Consider freewriting, letting your character run amok.*

- *If you are finding it hard to get into your project, try writing in a new blank document.*

- *If your writing time turns sour, take a break, set the material aside, and work on something else.*

- *Overcommitting to writing can load on added stress. Set smaller daily goals.*

- *Use weird time and mundane time to your advantage.*

- *Consider getting as many activities as you can into routine or habit. That will free up time for writing and streamline your life.*

- *Consider tracking all you do each day for a week. See where time is wasted, identify your habits, and think of ways to turn activities into routines for more time efficiency.*

# Chapter 10: Getting to the Core of Your Distractions

We took a look at distractions a bit in an earlier chapter, but I want to go deeper into this topic. We all know what things distract us during the day and what our "weaknesses" are. Some of us just can't stay off social media or check our phones for messages or emails every five minutes. Others get partway through writing a page and notice the floor needs sweeping or the dirty dishes are sitting in the sink.

One prolific best-selling suspense writer I know says she will find every and any reason not to write. She'll be on her hands and knees scrubbing the stain out of her carpet instead of working on her scene. She looks for excuses to not write.

That's not because she hates writing. It's because writing novels is hard!

It takes intense focus and concentration, and the effort is often mentally exhausting. And again, if we're pushing ourselves to write difficult scenes because of a deadline (self-imposed or no) and/or we're trying to be productive during a low time biologically, we are going to be more easily distracted.

It takes a lot of discipline to stick your butt in your chair, stay there, and be focused so you can crank out those scenes.

This is one reason I go to the library to write many of my novels' scenes. I love my house—I'm in the woods on a creek and have a big porch with a table that looks out over the beautiful scenery. You'd think I would write here all the time.

I often do, but when I really need to eliminate as many distractions as possible, I leave. Because the floor does need sweeping, the dishes need washing, and the dog needs to play ball (like, every hour).

So putting yourself in a place where the distractions are limited is a great help.

And understanding why you get distracted is half the battle.

## The Why of Distraction

Studies show that in the office, nearly 50% of US employees say they work for only fifteen minutes before getting distracted, and 53% report that they waste an hour or more each day due to disruptions.

These distractions can vary from noise to heavy workload and deadline pressure to feeling fatigued. And some studies have found that men have a harder time than women when it comes to focusing and are more inclined to suffer from wandering attention spans (surprised?).

Our brain structure may be to blame for some of this wandering. The prefrontal cortex of the brain regulates attention span and handles our emotions. So the rise of strong emotions (frustration, anger, annoyance) can cause us to be distracted from concentration.

The first step in all this is to zoom in and pinpoint the particular problem that is causing the distraction.

If we're distracted because of a strong emotion, we may need to deal with the situation causing the emotion before we can hunker down and write. Even if it means yelling in the closet for ten minutes, then shelving the emotion temporarily. We all have problems that crop up in life that cause emotional distress and that aren't easily resolved. That's life.

## Big Tasks Are Daunting

In fact, they can be so daunting they freeze us up. I think that's what most writer's block is about. The blank screen isn't just one blank page to us; it represents the whole darn book we're trying to write. We're staring at an elephant and not a mouse, and that elephant is just too big to take in.

Solution? Break up the task, even if just in your mind, into smaller tasks. That's why I set about writing one scene a day. I can do one scene. I've written one scene in a day plenty of times. It's a doable task for me. If I sit down and think about how many more scenes I need to write before I'm done, I may not start.

That's why I love putting my scenes on index cards. I sit down at my computer to write, pull the top card out of the rubber-banded stack, and start writing. Some days I'll write ten scenes. But I don't ever start with that goal.

I honestly believe this is a main reason writers procrastinate. The job is just too overwhelming. It's too big a task. When you've written a dozen or more novels, you know you'll get to the end. You know it's just a matter of one scene after the other and, before long, you'll be done. But if you've never written a full-length book, the finish line seems halfway across the globe. It feels like a marathon.

Thing is, it is a marathon. But with a big difference.

I mentioned the fable of the tortoise and the hare in the first chapter of this book. Slow and steady wins the race, right? I know, when I sit down to write the first scene of a new novel, that if I think about the marathon ahead, I'll start sweating. I'll probably notice how dirty the floor is and get out the mop.

But if I remind myself that those slow and steady steps have always gotten me to the finish line, I'll take the first steps. Remember the famous line from Lao Tzu: a journey of a thousand miles begins with a single step. Don't focus on the thousand miles. Just look at the path directly in front of you and start walking.

## Consider Compartmentalizing Tasks

Here's another hack I use. I'll list all those things I want to get done over a week, and they're usually big projects I'm working on (writing and editing). I know myself well enough to realize that if I work on just one project to the exclusion of all others, I'll get distracted. I'll be thinking about that editing job I'm late starting. Or those blog posts I must get written for my blog.

So I'll allocate compartments of time during a day so that I get some work done on multiple projects. For instance, I might decide to put in two hours on my novel, one hour writing blog posts, one hour to do two email blasts, two hours for a client's critique, and two hours editing for another client. When the thought pops up "You really have to get that guest post done for Angela," I can mollify my rippling anxiety by reminding myself: "You've put that on Friday's schedule. So forget about it." And, guess what? I do!

What this hack results in is a sum total of accomplishments at the end of the week that would still get accomplished if I did them one at a time, start to finish. But the difference is this: if I do them one at a time, I will have to fight distraction and guilt and grumpiness the whole week because the pressure of not making progress on all those other things will eat at me. And my productivity and quality of work will be affected.

Conversely, at the end of each day, I can look at all those projects I made headway on, knowing by the end of the week I'll have met my goals. I feel great when I complete all those little compartmentalized projects. Yes, they're only partially done each day. But I know my personality, and I like juggling a lot of different things. And I get antsy and bored if I spend too many hours in one day on one thing.

That's how I am. You may be different. But if this sounds like something that would work for you, give it a try. Set a timer. When that hour is up, leave it, take a break, then jump into the next compartment.

It can be fun too. And when you pick up the next day where you left off in your writing, you're chomping at the bit—because you stopped right in the middle of something and know how to pick it up and get running.

### Messy Desk

What else distracts you when you're trying to write? I talked about turning off notifications and unplugging your phone. But what about your work environment? Is your desk area a mess? Does that distract you?

Some people thrive in chaos, so if that's you, cleaning up your work area isn't going to help you be productive. But if you're the type that finds her eyes wandering to those sticky notes dangling from your computer monitor or the photos on the wall of your grandkids (or that jar of Hershey's Kisses), maybe it would be a good idea to clear them out of your sight. This is a little thing, but it could make a difference in your concentration.

What about music? Does that help or hinder you when you write? I know one author who selects specific movie soundtracks to listen to when he writes. If he's working on a high-action, tense suspense scene, he'll choose music to fit that. It gets him "in the mood."

Music, and just about any noise, distracts me, as I mentioned earlier, so I turn off everything I can when I'm writing. However, the sound of the rain pattering and the creek gurgling outside my window is soothing and helps my mood.

## Reward Yourself

Just as with those hacks, distractions can be a mind game. So if you're prone to being easily distracted, why not bribe yourself to work up the motivation to best them? Tell yourself if you focus and write three pages, you can then get up and grab a piece of chocolate. I have multiple jars of chocolate in my house. When I get through writing a challenging passage, I'll give myself permission to eat some chocolate.

If you have serious eating disorders, this might not be a good idea. But I think a lot of people find a reward system motivating. I'm sure this has to do with our childhood. "If you're good and sit there quietly, Mommy will buy you an ice cream, Johnny." I know—we're all grown up now and shouldn't have to stay stuck in that reward behavior mentality.

But it works. It feels good to reward yourself when you've accomplished something. We too often storm ahead on projects without stopping to pat ourselves on the back.

Be nice to yourself. Soak in that good feeling of pride and satisfaction when you finish writing a scene. That, to me, is the best part of writing! Even if the scene still needs a lot of work, instead of looking at the flaws, be glad you got the scene roughed in and written down.

This goes back to the A in the Productivity ABCs—you have to work on that uplifting self-talk. Don't focus on the negative and what you didn't get done or what's bad about your writing. You've learned that negativity is a productivity killer. And it's *distracting*.

## Other Ways to Cut Down on Distractions

Take those little breaks. As I previously mentioned, concentrating hard is tiring, so give yourself a five- or ten-minute break every hour. Stand, stretch, grab a snack, wash a few dishes, play with the dog.

If you do have to work in a noisy environment, consider getting headphones. Either snuff out the noise or play some music (if that helps) or white noise. I log on to Simplynoise.com and choose the type of noise color (yes, there are varieties of noise) I want to listen to, then crank it up. I prefer the lower tones to the higher ones. Also, when people see you in Starbucks, for example, with headphones on, they're less likely to bug you and start up a conversation.

Think about what distracts you. Make a list (sometimes making lists is a distraction!) of everything you can think of that distracts you when you're trying to write, then work to eliminate those distractions. Create a "Stop Doing" list and then work to cross those items off your list.

I mentioned how I often go to my local library to write tough scenes because I am so easily distracted, and I will stop and clean my floor instead of write. I still have to fight the urge to wander onto the Internet, but I'm not willing to set up apps to prevent me from doing so. If I ever get that out of control and can't rein in my wandering, I'll consider lockdown.

Only you know your habits and choices and attitudes. The purpose of this book is to help you examine your ABCs and through that process make some new, different choices so that you'll be super productive.

*Let's review:*

- *Understanding why we get distracted at any particular time can help us hack around that.*

- *Some distractions are caused by emotional issues that we might need to take care of first before being able to concentrate on writing.*

- *Big tasks (like writing a book) are daunting, so break up the tasks into bite-sized pieces.*

- *Consider compartmentalizing tasks and assigning periods of time each day to work on a variety of tasks to feel a sense of accomplishment.*

- *If mess distracts you, clean up your workspace. If music helps you concentrate, turn it on.*

- *Reward yourself when you get your writing done. Rewards can be great motivators.*

- *Make a list of the things that distract you, then come up with hacks to get around them.*

- *Identifying your habits, assessing which ones help and which ones hinder your productivity, and making new habits is the key to success.*

# Chapter 11: Thwarting Self-Sabotage

"I do nothing upon myself, and yet I am my own executioner."

—John Dunne

I've perhaps saved the biggest issue for last, for, honestly, we are our own worst enemies, and I believe self-sabotage, more than anything else, keeps us from being super-productive writers.

We've taken a look at a lot of attitude topics and discussed ways to think positively, boost ourselves with uplifting self-talk, and use mental hacks to adjust our attitudes.

But even if you correct all your bad habits, optimize your writing time, and adjust your schedule to fit your biology, if you have a tendency to self-sabotage, all your good effort may be for naught.

So we're going to take a look at some of the reasons and ways we self-sabotage and consider some remedies to help us thwart those destructive attitudes and behaviors.

Some studies have shown that self-sabotage leads to cycles of negative motivation. Meaning, the more you engage in self-sabotage, the less motivated you are to get something done. It's a self-perpetuating cycle that will prevent you from ever being truly productive.

Each time you fail, you prove to yourself that you just can't accomplish your task. If you sit down to write and tell yourself it's going to suck or you'll never get the scene written, you'll fulfill your own prophecy. And the next time you sit down, all you have to do is pull out the proof from previous attempts to discourage you from trying again. And when you do finally push through to write, the results are pathetic, due to the pressure you are heaping on your head.

# Self-Sabotage Cycles

Many of us fall into the trap of self-sabotage cycles, which pushes us to underperform. We know how tenacious habits are and how difficult they are to change. In order to break free from self-sabotage cycles, we will have to be determined and stalwart, like the heroes in our novels.

Simply stated, self-sabotage is any behavior, mind-set, emotion, or action that holds you back from getting or doing what you want, and it's usually subconscious. Because of our past, we opt for these habits because they act as a safety mechanism to keep us from suffering disappointment or depression. Our brains are doing what they are supposed to: protecting us from harm and keeping us comfortable.

If every time we jumped up out of our bunk bed we hit our head on a low ceiling, our brain would start warning us before we threw off the covers each morning. We would develop a habit rather quickly of pausing and carefully extricating ourselves from the bed instead of leaping upward. Our brain has our best interests in mind (does that sound as weird to you as it does to me?).

But, ultimately, our brain is not doing us any favors.

We find ourselves at times intentionally impeding our own progress when we're trying to get writing done. This isn't just about those moments when we stop writing to sweep the floor. There's a difference between hacking through distractions or inner resistance to writing and actually self-sabotaging—which is more entrenched and virulent.

Self-sabotage has deep roots in feelings of low self-esteem, self-worth, and self-confidence. I would venture to say we all struggle with these attitudes at various times and on various levels. What makes them so challenging to thwart is they have developed over years of life, and every time we've failed and been ridiculed or someone has made us feel "less than," those negative self-feelings hardened just a little more.

Now we have a concrete wall in front of us that we have to sledge-hammer through, and it's not an easy task.

## Types of Self-Sabotage

We each have concocted a unique cocktail of self-sabotage, which might be made up of some of the following ingredients:

- Fear of taking risks
- Fear of making mistakes
- Fear of failing
- Inability to say no
- Inability to make firm plans
- Inability to listen well
- Inability to consider the consequences of our actions
- Inability to think clearly when trying to make a decision
- Inability to admit mistakes
- Tendency to complain about others or blame them
- Tendency to worry excessively
- Tendency to procrastinate
- Tendency to have unrealistic expectations
- Tendency to judge others harshly
- Expecting ourselves to be perfect
- Excessive time spent daydreaming or engaged in wishful thinking
- Tendency to compare ourselves with others

These components that contribute to self-sabotage manifest in thoughts like "I can't do this" or "This will never work."

Here are three helpful ways to interrupt the cycle of self-sabotage:

1. *Identify the bad behavior.* The first step in beating self-sabotage is catching ourselves doing it. Stop and sit down, pick up pen and paper, and begin listing the inner dialogue—those statements we make and those tendencies we have that are preventing us from being productive.

Try to pinpoint specific triggers that launch these behaviors. They could be people, objects, situations, places, or even times of day. Sometimes we can remove the triggers. For instance, if we tend to self-sabotage when we sit down to write at the kitchen table—because we give in to distractions as excuses not to write—we can pack up our laptop and head to the public library. Other times, we can't remove the triggers, so in those instances we need to understand how they're functioning.

Ask yourself questions:

- What am I believing about this situation that is sabotaging me?
- What is this causing me to believe about myself and my abilities?
- How did this belief trigger my self-sabotage pattern?
- How is this belief ridiculous and self-destructive?
- What is a healthier, kinder perspective I could adopt?

2. *Create Healthy Alternate Behavior.* Hey, we're writers—we should be able to come up with some creative alternatives to bad behavior. In order to eliminate the bad, we need to replace it with the good. With behavior that's helpful and encouraging. We can't always avoid people, situations, or objects that cause us to react in detrimental ways. So we need to list things that answer these questions:

- What's a better and more appropriate way I could respond to this trigger that would help me break out of this self-sabotage cycle?

- How will I benefit from responding this way instead of the former way?

- What is the key advantage for changing this behavior?

3. *Practice Makes Better.* Or, better said: practice turns into habit. Every time your triggers fire and you begin to self-sabotage, stop and run through your challenging questions, reminding yourself of why and how you want to change the reaction to that trigger. The more you stop yourself and replace the old attitude with the new, the sooner that new behavior will be a habit. This goes beyond the self-talk we discussed in the early chapters of this book—because habits of self-sabotage are so deeply ingrained.

Sure, this will take work and time, but every little victory is a step forward and away from the debilitating habits of self-sabotage.

Take time each day to reflect on your progress, to learn from your mistakes. Look at the big goal of a lifestyle and attitude change that will stretch over the course of your life. It takes courage to expand our perspective, to get out of our small ruts and limited thinking. But it's worth it.

If possible, enlist others to help you. It's no fun at all to have someone point out to you those moments you slip into self-sabotage, but if you can keep from getting defensive, this can help so much. We often can't spot our own destructive attitudes and behavior. Ask your family members or friends to speak up in kindness and love, not criticism. Or you could come up with a signal of some sort to imply "you are doing it again." Maybe they can make a goofy face or give a gesture like pulling their hair out. If it can make you laugh instead of get angry, that's going to motivate you more to change the bad behavior.

I like the idea of rewarding yourself when you spot and stop a trigger. If you make this "seek and destroy" activity a fun and challenging one, it may make it easier to replace and turn the bad into good habits. Chocolate, anyone?

**Some Great Hacks for Bypassing Self-Sabotage**

While you're working hard at identifying those triggers and changing them into positive habits, adopting a few helpful hacks might aid you to get your writing done. While we've looked at these before, they are great hacks to work around the sabotaging tendencies.

- *Set the timer and just go for it.* Push through the negative self-talk and fears of failure and need to be perfect and make yourself write for fifteen minutes without stopping to edit, criticize, reread, or make excuses. Just do it.

- *Use the two-minute rule.* If you can't write for even fifteen minutes, give yourself two minutes to do something, such as write the first line of your scene. It's easy to get quickie tasks done and out of the way, and while it may not produce a huge sense of accomplishment, it's a way of starting when you are in freeze mode. It bears repeating that big, daunting tasks paralyze us. So instead of sitting down and thinking how we have a huge book to write, focusing on getting one sentence or one paragraph done isn't intimidating. And we'll often find that once the two minutes is up, we want to keep writing.

- *Change your environment.* Certain colors are soothing; others are unnerving. This goes for smells and sounds as well. Think about the temperature in your work environment. I can't tell you how many times I've had to leave a Starbucks or the library because it's just too darn cold for me. Something as simple as that could be interfering with your concentration and triggering those self-sabotaging behaviors.

## A Word about Expectations

If we hold unreasonable expectations of ourselves, failure to meet those expectations can demoralize us and send us headlong into that cycle of self-sabotage. It would be helpful, if you're struggling with these issues, to examine your expectations.

If you're expecting perfection every time you sit down to write (and we'll be looking at perfectionism next), you will never meet your expectations, and you'll sabotage your future attempts at writing.

If sitting down, in itself, is a trigger to self-sabotage, you have some work to do. I have a few friends who've been talking about writing their book for years. But every single time they sit down to write, regardless of how well prepared they are to get the words onto the page, their cycle of sabotage is triggered. Just the act of sitting in the chair and opening up a blank Word document sends them into paralysis due to the dialogue triggered in their head.

They long to write. They have so much they want to say. But they can't rewire the triggers. All the coaxing from friends seems to fall on deaf ears. Ultimately, only they can work through this, and only if they really want to.

It could be their expectations are way too high. Instead of thinking they have to get a whole chapter done, it might help to aim for one page of rough material. Just getting something down on the page can help break a stubborn trigger.

*Let's review:*

- *Self-sabotage is highly ingrained, and we tend to develop these cycles unconsciously.*

- *The long-term effects of self-sabotage create negative motivation, which leads to lower productivity.*

- *Self-sabotage is a way of protecting ourselves from disappointment and depression, but in the long run it's hurting us.*

- *There are many different types of self-sabotaging, and we need to identify which ones we succumb to and try to stop them.*

- *One good way to stop self-sabotaging is through identifying the triggers that cause the behavior and then rewiring them into positive, helpful habits.*

- *Using some hacks can help us retrain our brains to stop self-sabotaging.*

- *We need to adopt reasonable expectations for what we can accomplish so that we don't reinforce the cycle of self-sabotage.*

# Chapter 12: Perfectionism Is the Perfect Self-Sabotage

You sit down to write. Finally, you found some time to work on your book. You feel prepared; you've thought through the scene or talking point you want to tackle today. You've cleared your plate—the kids are at school, the dishes are done, and you've dealt with your email.

But as you open your Word doc on your computer and your fingers hover over the keyboard, a sense of unease trickles in.

The eager anticipation starts to feel like dread, and the doubts form into excuses. "Maybe I need to think through this scene a bit more." Or "I probably should do a bit more research before I start." Or, even worse: "It's going to suck."

And those thoughts trigger all those familiar feelings.

Doubt. Irritation. Depression. Hopelessness.

All over the thought of writing a chapter in your book that won't be perfect.

This type of perfectionist behavior is common self-sabotage. But why do so many of us slip into this way of thinking?

I spoke in previous chapters about some effective hacks we can adopt to get past our resistance to writing. And while we each can conjure up some great hacks that get our minds and motivation on track, if we succumb to the trappings of perfectionism, those hacks may fall as flat as pancakes on the floor of our determination to be productive.

There are many ways we self-sabotage our writing productivity (among, perhaps, many other things we attempt to accomplish), and perfectionism is especially heinous.

# The Need for Perfectionism Has Various Causes

I want to take a hard look at perfectionism because it has numerous sources, and identifying the source(s) of your perfectionism (or apparent perfectionism) might help you squash it.

Is perfectionism a bad thing?

Good question. I think having some desire to create the perfect scene or nonfiction chapter can be positively motivating. Healthy striving to reach higher and better benchmarks presses us toward excellence.

But something bad happens when we feel we must be perfect and failure equates with worthlessness.

Basically, here are the differences between healthy striving and perfectionism according to the University of Texas (Austin) Mental Health Center:

## Perfectionism

- Setting standards beyond reach and reason
- Never being satisfied by anything less than perfection
- Becoming depressed when faced with failure or disappointment
- Being preoccupied with fears of failure and disapproval
- Seeing mistakes as evidence of unworthiness
- Becoming overly defensive when criticized

## Healthy Striving

- Setting standards that are high but within reach
- Enjoying process as well as outcome
- Bouncing back quickly from failure or disappointment
- Keeping normal anxiety and fear of failure within bounds

- Seeing mistakes as opportunities for growth and learning

- Reacting positively to helpful criticism

It's a myth to believe perfectionists accomplish more than non-perfectionists. In fact, because of the insecurity pressing perfectionists, they often give in to procrastination, miss deadlines, and suffer low productivity. They tend to be "all or nothing" thinkers, and that type of mind-set can cause overwhelm.

When a perfectionist accomplishes something, it's usually in spite of her perfectionism, not because of it.

### Learn from Joseph Grand's Mistake

I remember studying Camus's *The Plague* in high school, and the discussion in class still lingers in my ear.

Joseph Grand, a clerk in the municipal government, confesses to Dr. Bernard Rieux, the narrator of the story, that he is writing a "book or something of the sort." When Rieux asks Grand if he is "getting good results," Grand answers, "Well, yes, I think I'm making headway."

Rieux then asks, "Have you much more to do?" to which Grand responds, "That's not the point . . . I can assure you that's not the point."

What does Grand want? He wants his manuscript to be "flawless."

Anne Lamott says in her wonderful book *Bird by Bird* about aspiring writers:

"They kind of want to write, but they really want to be published." However, she notes, "Publication is not all that it is cracked up to be. But writing is."

In the quest of a "flawless" manuscript, Grand encounters troubles.

"Evenings, whole weeks, spent on one word, just think! Sometimes on a mere conjunction! I'd like you to understand, Doctor, I grant you it's easy enough to choose between a 'but' and an 'and.' It's a bit more difficult to decide between 'and' and 'then.' But definitely the hardest thing may be to know whether one should put an 'and' or leave it out."

To this, the unflappable Dr. Rieux responds, "Yes, I see your point."

As the story unfolds, we learn that Grand aspires to write the perfect sentence. And it becomes apparent to the reader that the "book or something of the sort" consists of exactly this single sentence:

"One fine morning in the month of May an elegant young horsewoman might have been seen riding a handsome sorrel mare along the flowery avenues of the Bois de Bologne."

He works on this sentence throughout the story. Needless to say, he doesn't get very far. And his book never gets written.

## Perfectionism: "The Voice of the Oppressor"

Lamott also says, "Perfectionism is the voice of the oppressor. . . . It will keep you cramped and insane your whole life, and it is the main obstacle between you and a shitty first draft. . . . [It] will ruin your writing, blocking inventiveness and playfulness and life force. . . . Perfectionism means that you try desperately not to leave so much mess to clean up. But clutter and mess show us that life is being lived."

True. Perfectionism oppresses. But let's take another look at why perfectionism is a bad thing.

## Perfectionism Is Bad for Your Health

Perfectionism takes its toll on our health, mentally and physically. Chronic worry and discouragement not only kills our joy of living but also leads to an exhausted state. It infects those around us too, putting a strain on relationships. The constant stress caused by perfectionism eventually leads to problems such as weakened immunity, digestive problems, and insomnia.

Perfectionism exaggerates the importance or value of what you're trying to achieve. Seriously, you're only attempting to write a book, not save the world. If you don't write the perfect book, thousands aren't going to die. The stress of putting too much importance on your tasks, whatever they may be, can make you sick over the long run.

Perfectionism seeps into the psyche and creates a pervasive personality type. It reduces playfulness and the assimilation of knowledge, because if you're always focused on your own performance and on defending yourself, you can't focus on learning a task.

If we're in the habit of expecting perfection from ourselves, our creativity and innovation are at risk of being squelched. We sabotage our ability to write our best book. And our energy is drained in the process.

## Perfectionism in the Guise of Procrastination

Is it possible your obsession with perfectionism is actually an excuse to procrastinate? Maybe fear is at the heart of your perfectionism.

If we fear we will fail and, as a result, face rejection, jeering, and humiliation, procrastination is a safe course of action. But we don't want to admit we're procrastinating, so we mask it in the guise of perfectionism.

I asked my readers what keeps them from starting or finishing their manuscript, and many told me they are afraid of failing, that there are hounded by perfectionism.

They know it's unreasonable to expect perfection in the material they write, yet they can't get past the belief their book has to be perfect before they can show it to anyone or release it into the world of readers.

Perfectionism can be difficult to identify. How do you know if you are truly a perfectionist?

Well, perfectionists tend to focus on product to the exclusion of the process.

Instead of enjoying the act of writing, their thoughts are fixated on the end result. Instead of accepting that a draft may start off awful and go through numerous iterations, a perfectionist will self-sabotage with the knowledge that whatever he writes won't be good enough.

Good enough for whom? It doesn't matter. It won't be good enough for someone.

Here are some characteristics of a perfectionist belief system:

- You are not okay as you are.

- No matter what you achieve, the feelings of satisfaction are temporary. There is always more to do, be, accomplish.

- Things are either black or white. Things in your life are either right or wrong, good or bad, successes or failures.

- You believe that if you make everything perfect on the outside, you will be at peace on the inside.

- If you continually achieve and acquire, you will be successful and happy.

- When things go wrong or you do not achieve at a certain level, you believe you have failed.

- Effort and intention aren't satisfying in themselves. If the results of your efforts aren't successful, you have no joy.

- You are competitive about almost everything.

- You feel judgmental of people who fall short of perfection.

- You imagine others admire and value you only for your high level of achievement and production.


Perfectionists are often high achievers, and even when they achieve, those feelings of satisfaction are temporary because they believe there is always more to do, be, or accomplish.

# Perfect Is Never Good Enough

Perfectionists are their own harshest critics, frequently berating themselves over any small thing that's just not right. They tend to do things in fits and starts, but end up discouraged and exhausted.

I've had a fascination for years with those who attempt to crest Mt. Everest. Honestly, these people, for the most part, are the most obsessed and crazy individuals. They are perfectionists who have to climb that mountain not "because it's there" but because they have to prove to themselves they are worthy or have value.

I've watched footage of many who failed to reach the top. They collapse in utter failure. Their lives are worthless. They may as well have died in the attempt, they seem to think. Making it up to fifty feet from the top is wholly unacceptable. There is no sense of accomplishment or victory or pride. It's failure, plain and simple.

It's not just a case of being competitive when these climbers have to go back and do it again and again. Sure, some may be driven competitively to make the peak more times than anyone else. Or be the first ___ (you fill in the blank) to ever climb Everest.

This unreasonable striving for perfection stems from a sense of self-worth that hinges on the expectations or approval of others. It is often referred to as "the highest form of self-abuse" because perfection doesn't actually exist.

Are you striving for perfection because anything less means you "are less"? Something to consider.

The sooner you come to grips with the truth that you aren't your art—your self-worth isn't connected in any way with what you create and how that creation is received by others—the sooner you'll break those chains of perfectionism.

I know, it's hard. Really hard.

Bad reviews can make us feel worthless. But we have to learn to separate truth from fiction.

Instead of wallowing in self-pity and doubt when we receive valid criticism (and I'm emphasizing *valid* because, well, writers can get a lot of dumb criticism that isn't helpful or valid at all), we need to step back with a professional attitude and see what ways we might improve our craft so our next attempt will be more successful and favorably received by readers.

## Thick Skin Needed

We writers need to develop a thick skin. Not so thick that we stubbornly refuse to take helpful criticism or instruction. But thick enough to throw off the slings and arrows of unhelpful criticism.

Just today I got an email from a reader who gave me a list of things I should have done differently in my latest novel. Things that were character choices, such as insisting a character should have moved an item from one hand to another before offering to shake hands. Or how she should have put down her violin before hugging her arms around herself (on the damp, cold grass late at night? I wondered).

This reader suggested I had a lot of wrong syntax and mistaken words, but those were true to my characters' education, background, and vocation (cowboys in the 1870s really did speak differently than we do in the US in the year 2017).

All this to say: if you're a writer who puts her work out for the world to read, you're going to get bad reviews, complaints, criticism, and—as this email demonstrates—readers who feel you should have written your story differently.

I recall how my mother, sole writer for the TV soap *The Doctors* (back in the '60s), used to get scathing, hateful mail from fans when she killed a character off or when some character broke up with another or cheated on her. She'd laugh and shrug and tell me, "You can't please everyone."

Good criticism should be welcomed, though.

I appreciate it when a reader points out some glaring mistake I made in one of my books. I thank the person and make the correction pronto.

But writers need to distinguish between helpful criticism and personal taste.

You can't please all the people all the time. If you have to get that novel just perfect so you'll never get a bad review, you need to develop a thicker skin. You need to stop procrastinating because of fear of failure.

*Let's review:*

- *The need to be perfect has various causes, and there's a difference between perfectionism and healthy striving.*

- *Perfectionism is an oppressor, and is can be detrimental for your health.*

- *Fear of failure and procrastination can manifest as a desire for perfection, and it's important to distinguish between procrastination and perfectionism.*

- *We need to separate our self-worth from our accomplishments. We are not what we accomplish.*

- *Writers need to be open to criticism but also develop a thick skin, knowing they will never please all the people all the time.*

# Chapter 13: How Procrastination Fits In with Perfectionism

Procrastination is often a *symptom* of perfectionism. Perfectionists, believing they can never complete a task perfectly, put it off as long as possible.

If a writer doesn't attempt to finish her project, she can't fail. She won't be ridiculed or get bad reviews that will break her heart. The greater the fear of criticism, the more she will procrastinate.

Some people think procrastinators are plain lazy. They're making excuses not to write because writing is hard. Well, many of us have moments when we feel that way.

I talked about this as well, in previous chapters. We stare at the computer screen, and out of the corner of our eye, we notice the floor is dirty. We jump up and grab the mop, telling ourselves we won't be able to concentrate on writing if the floor is dirty.

This isn't necessarily laziness.

Granted, some writers are lazy, and that's why they procrastinate. They like the idea of being an author, but they don't really want to put in the hard work of cranking out great books. They may tinker with writing the way they toy with many activities in their life. Everything is a hobby to dabble in. But dabbling does not a super-productive writer make.

The perfectionist procrastinates because she doesn't want to suffer the imagined pain that will come along with her perceived failure.

And there may be good reason for her to think this way.

She may have grown up with a lot of criticism. With parents who had ridiculously high expectations of her and put pressure on her to excel (even to be perfect). Every time she tried to please her parents, she failed, and those mean, disparaging words they uttered still burn like a hot brand on her heart.

Just knowing why you are a perfectionist doesn't make it go away. I get that. It's a lifelong struggle for some of us.

Some of us spend the first twenty or so years of our lives getting all screwed up by our parents, then spend the rest of our lives trying to undo all the damage they caused. If you had great, supportive parents that didn't mess you up, thank the heavens for that.

## How Can You Hack Around That?

Let's start looking at ways we can hack around some of these mind-sets.

Some research has concluded that people procrastinate when they view concrete tasks in abstract terms. There's this big, scary, massive novel waiting to be written, and the finish line is somewhere out on the horizon, far away and unreachable.

One of the hacks we looked at previously centered on breaking down the big task of writing a book into small pieces. Setting smaller goals for your writing time—ones that aren't daunting. Ones you can allow some imperfection to slip in.

## Perfect Is Relative

Who sets your standard of perfection? I mean, when you finish that book, who is the big scary judge out there just waiting to pounce on your project and tell you it sucks?

It's one thing to learn or know that your book could be better, could stand for some improvement. But you do know that no book, no *anything*, is ever perfect. Because there is no one standard that sets the definition of *perfect.*

Perfect is relative. It's subjective. It's a matter of opinion. Whose opinions are you going to listen to and why? And will you be willing to accept the opinions of those you hold in high regard?

I like the ancient Greek meaning of the word *perfect*: having reached its end; complete.

If we understand that perfection is really just completion, to the best of our ability, it can take some of the pressure off.

Some writers have given their book to a critique partner or group, or published it, only to get harsh negative feedback. And rather than be motivated by that criticism to improve their craft and write better books, they slip into the trap of perfectionism.

Criticism hurts, so it makes sense that we'd be afraid to write another book or finish our current book because we don't want to go through that again. So no way will we move forward because the book has to be perfect, and we know it never will be.

It's true—an artist who puts his work out into the world has to have the backbone to face the critics. Some people just can't seem to develop that strong a backbone. Some writers would rather not write or not finish their book because they can't bear the thought that someone (or many someones) will hate what they write.

There are ways to work through this, and I believe the best is to get the help of a supportive writing coach (either one-on-one or in a group setting). A writing coach can honestly point out your strengths and weaknesses and give you tools and insights to help you gain mastery of your craft, which instills confidence and can help you break through the trappings of perfectionism.

## How We Can Counteract Perfectionism

In addition to having supportive, concrete help with our writing, we can go back to that self-talk we covered in an earlier chapter.

If you catch yourself thinking in these perfectionist ways, you can do an exercise to help you put your fears in perspective.

Write down what you think are the worst things that might happen if you publish your book. Then next to each consequence you listed, write what subsequent results you fear most will develop from those. Then write a more realistic scenario and offer yourself practical next steps.

Here's an example:

If I publish my book, I'll get terrible reviews.

If I get terrible reviews, everyone I know will laugh at me or gossip about my awful writing behind my back. They'll unfriend me on Facebook and refuse to have lunch with me. I'll have to change my name and move to a new town.

[This is where you let your paranoid fantasies run loose. Just let them all out.]

If I get terrible reviews, I'll feel yucky for a while, but it's not the end of the world. Probably no one I know will even read the reviews. Or if they do, they aren't going to make fun of me. And if they do, they aren't really my friends, right?

So, I'll read the reviews and see what specifics are addressed. Then I'll find a professional editor or writing coach, or ask some trusted author friends for help, so I can improve in any weak areas. I'll find some books and blog posts and work on the main weaknesses in my writing.

I also know that a bad review doesn't mean I am a bad writer. Reviews are subjective, and what one reader hates, another reader may like. If a lot of reviewers complain about the same issues, then that gives me some good ideas of what I should work on. That's a good thing.

Let go of your desire to impress others. Understand the difference between excellence and perfection. You can learn to write an excellent book—but never a perfect one. Demanding perfection generates negative feelings from any perceived mistakes made instead of celebrating the effort put in.

## Some Other Ways to Combat Perfectionism

When you worry if what you're writing will be "good enough," here are some tips to help your brain change the self-talk:

*Don't wait for conditions to be perfect to get into your writing.* Accept that whatever you write will never be perfect. Go for "complete." Finish a scene or chapter. Let yourself feel the satisfaction of completion even while knowing your writing may need more work.

Instead of focusing on the finished product, *try adopting the five steps of design thinking*: discovery, interpretation, ideation, experimentation, and evolution.

I can't emphasize enough how important it is to enjoy the journey. "Life is a journey, not a destination." This is a saying that is hard for perfectionists to embrace. But if you are thinking only of the impossible destination, you won't experience the joy of the process. You will hate your writing time, and then you'll ask yourself: Why am I even writing in the first place?

## More Coping Strategies for Perfectionism

- *Make a list of the advantages and disadvantages of trying to be perfect.*
  Taking a look at the advantages vs. the disadvantages may help you see problems you may have with relationships, your work habits, eating and/or substance abuse issues, or any other compulsive behaviors and negative emotions. When you look at how those disadvantages outweigh the advantages, that might motivate you to fight the need to be perfect.

- *Pay attention to your perfectionist thoughts.*
  When you find yourself criticizing a less-than-perfect bit of writing, make yourself stop and find good parts of your writing. Then ask: Is this really as awful as I think it is? Is it reasonably good for a first draft or first rewrite? If someone else wrote this, what would you say as honest encouragement to uplift and congratulate the writer? Be your own best friend. God knows we have enough forces trying to tear us down in life.

- *Be realistic about what you can accomplish.*
  By setting more realistic goals, you will come to find that "less than" results do not lead to horrible consequences. Writing that flawed passage is not the end of the world. Find reasons to celebrate the things you've improved on.

- *Learn healthy ways to deal with criticism.*
  Perfectionists often view criticism as a personal attack, which leads them to respond defensively. Learn to be more objective about criticism and about yourself. Remind yourself that failed attempts help us learn and grow, which helps us improve.

Remember that criticism is a natural thing from which to learn rather than something to be avoided. I wish I'd had honest, helpful criticism decades ago with my first novels.

### Mind Hacks for Perfectionists

I like the technique of telling yourself you're not really going to write that scene; you're just going to "play around with it."

Some scenes, to me, are daunting and easy to put off. I struggle with writing climaxes of my novels because I feel "the pressure is on." It should be on, for my characters, but I get a kind of performance anxiety because I believe everything is riding on creating the perfect climax to my story.

So a hack I've used at times (though I'm not a perfectionist by any means) is to tell myself this is just an exercise to get my scene ideas tested. As I shared earlier, I'll sometimes open a new Word doc and write the scene in there, telling myself it's really not "an official" scene for my book.

Just doing that frees up my fears of writing a sucky scene. And almost always I end up with a scene that turns out both surprisingly different from the one I thought I'd write and much better than expected. When I copy and paste the scene into my novel, I feel like I've cheated somehow, but in a good way.

You can hack around your perfectionism by telling yourself you're only experimenting.

And you can put your active procrastination to good use. While you're scrubbing the floor or folding laundry instead of doing the writing you planned to do, you can ideate.

A lot of great writers do this. They problem-solve, imagine scenes, and play around with character types—essentially getting a lot of the necessary work done to pave the way for great writing.

Toni Morrison said she did the hard work of thinking through her scenes while doing chores or other activities, so that when she sat down to write, she was ready to roll. Tony Hillerman likes to lie his couch with his eyes closed.

If perfectionism has you staring at the blank computer screen, that feeling of dread seeping in, preparation can take the edge of it—maybe even get you so excited about what your characters are about to do that you forget you're demanding perfection from yourself.

And what about asking friends and family to help you break out of perfectionism? Enlist their help. Tell them you are struggling with perfectionism, that you don't want vacuous accolades spurring you on to write or praising your material. Tell them you'd like them to hold you accountable to getting the work done, to keeping to your writing schedule.

## Don't Wait for the Perfect Moment

I always tell my kids to hurry up and have children. They keep waiting for the perfect moment, the perfect set of circumstances, to start or add to their family. Meanwhile, Grandma is not getting any younger, and she wants to enjoy watching her grandchildren grow.

When my husband and I started our family, we were broke, in school, and unskilled to enter the workforce, but that didn't stop us (ex-hippies that we were). We think back to those years, and, yes, they were hard at times, but we got by and found great joy in raising our children. If we'd waited for the perfect moment, we'd be childless to this day.

All this to say: there will never be a perfect moment to write. Well, maybe there will, on rare occasion—when all the elements of the universe align just right to allow you to be brilliant and create the perfect scene.

But if you can't write unless everything is perfect—the environment, the weather, your health, life in general—you'll never write.

Don't wait until inspiration lights you up. Ease into your writing. Sit and doodle if you have to. Journal or freewriting on a blank document on your computer. We looked at how freewriting can help inspire our scenes when we take on the voice of our characters and let them speak to us.

Find ways you can break through your need for perfectionism, then put them into practice.

### Get into the Habit of Doing instead of Thinking

Many people are great at talking about what they're going to do but have a world of trouble actually doing those things. They might have to spend hours or days talking themselves into writing before a word is written.

Practice doing things instead of thinking about them. The longer an idea sits in your head without being acted on, the weaker it becomes. After a few days the details get hazy. After a week it's completely forgotten. If you get an exciting idea and write it down, you may be able to stir up the excitement days later when you review your notes. But chances are much of your idea will have faded along with your enthusiasm.

I like the cliché: strike while the iron is hot (though I don't really get what it means). But I can picture being heated with a great idea—one I don't want to cool off before expanding it into a scene element or plot development.

Action helps cure fear. Sitting and mulling allows fear to build up. Getting into action diffuses that fear. Public speakers will tell you the hardest part of speaking is waiting to go on stage. Once they get rolling into their talk, the fear subsides.

## Work on Self-Love

The key point is that perfectionism grows from a point of feeling not only imperfect but deeply flawed and therefore unlovable. If you have to constantly re-earn or re-prove your worth—even if it's to yourself—you are running on a never-ending treadmill of external achievements that will never make you happy.

We need to embrace the fact that self-acceptance and peace do not come from changing what is outside. Remember, lasting change always entails focusing on what's inside of you. You can never hack your way into self-love. No matter what anyone has said to you and about you in the past, you are a valuable, worthy human being deserving of love and respect. We have to love ourselves before we can love others, and while that can be hard, it's the way to joy, health, and peace.

*Let's review:*

- *Procrastination can be a symptom of perfectionism.*

- *The concept of "perfect" is relative and subjective. By understanding that "complete" is easier to approach than "perfect," we can hack through to be productive.*

- *When you catch yourself thinking in perfectionist ways, stop and ask yourself key questions to rewire your thinking.*

- *Don't wait for conditions to be perfect to write; they never will be.*

- *Make a list of pros and cons of being perfect to help you see how perfectionism isn't truly helping you in achieving your goals.*

- *Be realistic with your goals.*

- *Adopt a healthy acceptance of criticism.*

- *Hack around your perfectionism by telling yourself you are only experimenting with writing.*

- *Don't wait for the perfect moment to write.*

- *Get into the habit of doing instead of thinking.*

- *Believe in your intrinsic value; you are worthy of love and, hence, self-love.*

# Chapter 14: The Life of a Super-Productive Writer

In this broad and deep look at the Productivity ABCs—attitude, biology, and choices—we've considered many of the roadblocks that keep us from "cranking it out."

Every writer is different and brings with him, into his writing life, a unique set of roadblocks. Only you can determine what those are, the ways that might work to crash through them or hack around them, and the lifelong adjustments you may need to make to become the super-productive writer you long to be.

## Who Is That Writer in the Mirror?

I want to talk about your self-image for a moment. In the introduction, I mentioned that you're not really an author in the professional or career sense until you publish a book. But even before you get "there," it's important to see that goal, that finish line.

If you haven't finished writing that first book, fix it in your mind that you're a productive writer. See yourself as a professional, not an amateur. Everything you do should be with that mind-set, and with the ultimate goal before you.

If you've already published a book or two, you still need to adjust your thinking. You want to be a highly successful, highly productive writer, so picture what that looks like. Can you imagine writing and publishing two or three books a year, every year? Maybe you envision five or six.

Whatever your ultimate dream is, let it be a positive thought and motivating force to get you there.

# Fear Not

I have editing clients who have written a few novels, but those manuscripts are just lingering in a folder on their computer. These writers are not taking those next steps to publish. This isn't an issue of money—waiting until they can pay to have the books edited.

This is really about fear. And fear leads to things like procrastination, making excuses, striving for "perfect," and succumbing to endless distractions.

One of the toughest and most important attitudes writers need to master is summed up in the famous words of Franklin Roosevelt: "The only thing we have to fear is fear itself."

When we work from a place of fear, it infects every aspect of our life.

I recall one of my high school teachers lecturing us graduating students, describing how most people go through life "content to taste the broth and never bite into the steak." That line stuck with me all these years, and it reminds me of another observation I heard somewhere: "Some people live for eighty years, but they're really only living the same year over and over eighty times." Which implies that those people aren't *really living*. They're not stretching themselves, taking risks, trying new things. They are doing the same old, same old, and, frankly, that's a sad thing.

Why do I say it's sad? Because life is short, and if we let fear hold us back from exploring all the many things we've longed to do, that's a tragedy.

I'm not talking about a bucket list here. Who wants to wait until she's old and feeble to climb Half Dome in Yosemite or drive cattle across Wyoming? Don't put off writing until you are too old (or dead) to write.

Maybe you don't think you have any fear when it comes to writing. But then, why aren't you cranking out books? Why aren't you super productive? I'm guessing it's because you're afraid of something.

## Just Too Busy to Write

I hear some of you saying, "I'm not afraid. I just have no time." Well, we've seen how that is often an excuse for not writing. We've seen how plenty of writers, working more than full-time, and some with huge challenges in their health or responsibilities, have carved out time to do what they love. Maybe they don't "crank" out books, but they do get their books written.

So if you're saying you have no time to write, and you're not making this excuse because you're just unmotivated to be a writer, then maybe it is fear. You may be afraid that if you co-opt time for writing, other areas of your life may suffer. Your family may end up hating you. Your husband will leave you. Your chores will pile up. You'll have a nervous breakdown.

I get all that. But these fears, grounded or not, have to be faced if you want to be a writer. Sure, it may take some time, some trial and error, to come up with a good schedule that won't adversely affect the rest of your life. And you may have to tweak that schedule from time to time. I do, all the time.

If you really want to be a productive writer, don't let those excuses stop you.

## If You Truly Can't Crank Out Books

I want to be clear here, again: some people have ginormous obstacles to being productive. They have health issues, or they're full-time caregivers, or they have mental, emotional, or situational challenges that are not easily conquered.

I hope, if you fall into this group, you've learned some helpful tips to maximize what precious little writing time you can steal away. I hope, if you're plagued with some of the aforementioned attitudes or habits, that you've learned some useful ways to best them to help make those brief writing experiences fulfilling.

My words to you are these. Find joy in those moments, but don't expect yourself to produce like those who have few valid excuses for not writing. Try to find a strong sense of fulfillment in the effort, and if you don't think you can crank out books in the near future, consider cranking out blog posts, which can be as short as three hundred words. Or crank out some short stories.

If writing is your passion, don't smother it. Eke out those moments to write, grabbing your "weird" time opportunities. You have insights and experiences to share through your writing, and you probably know better than I do how therapeutic and comforting writing can be. You have an audience waiting to hear what you have to say, so don't quit. Make writing, somehow and in some way, a part of your life.

## Make It So, Number One

When Captain Picard of the starship *Enterprise* was ready to zoom off on some mission, he would look at Commander Riker and say, "Make it so, Number One."

Every time you sit down to write, you are in the captain's chair, facing a wide-open, endless, limitless universe of potential. Isn't that thrilling? Think about it—the sky's the limit when it comes to writing. You can write *anything* you can imagine. Doesn't that excite you? That excites me!

As we age, we seem to lose our awe. We get sucked into the daily grind and weighted down by life's responsibilities. We forget what it feels like to throw off our shoes on a whim and run through a meadow barefoot. Or run off a dock and leap in the air, shivering as we splash down into the cold mountain lake water.

We can recapture the sense of awe whenever we sit down to write, if we would just tell ourselves, "Make it so, Number One."

It's all up to you to examine your Productivity ABCs and make the course corrections that will lead you to the stars and beyond. May you write long and prosper!

# About the Author

C. S. Lakin is passionate about writing and helping writers see success in their writing journey. She's the author of eighteen novels in various genres, which includes her seven-book fantasy series The Gates of Heaven and five novels in her historical Western romance Front Range series (under pen name Charlene Whitman). She works full-time as a copyeditor and writing coach.

Her award-winning blog for writers, Live Write Thrive, is an excellent resource for both fiction and nonfiction writers, with hundreds of posts on craft, marketing, and writing for life. She also puts out a newsletter to her readers with tips and insights on how to be productive and find success as a writer.

In addition to editing and proofreading, Lakin critiques more than two hundred manuscripts a year. If you've never had your work critiqued, you may be unaware of many weaknesses in your writing and story structure. Consider getting your scene outline or first chapters critiqued to help you see what needs work. You can learn more about her critique services at Critique My Manuscript.

If you're a novelist—or aspiring to be one—be sure to join her Novel Writing Fast Track email list. No participation necessary! You'll get two free ebooks on writing craft the first week, and can enter a Rafflecopter contest each month in which she gives away more free books, all to help you fast track to success. Contact Susanne at contact@livewritethrive.com to learn more.

**Did you find this book helpful?**
**Please take a minute to leave an honest review on Amazon!**
**It's the best way to say thank you to an author, and it will help other writers.**

**Don't miss the books in The Writer's Toolbox series!
These books cover nearly everything you need to
know to write great fiction and structure solid stories!**

*Writing the Heart of Your Story: The Secret to Crafting an
Unforgettable Novel*

*Shoot Your Novel: Cinematic Techniques to Supercharge Your
Writing*

*The 12 Key Pillars of Novel Construction: Your Blueprint for
Building a Solid Story*

*The 12 Key Pillars Workbook*

*5 Editors Tackle the 12 Fatal Flaws of Fiction Writing*

*Say What? The Fiction Writer's Handy Guide to Grammar,
Punctuation, and Word Usage*

*Layer Your Novel: The Innovative Method for Plotting Your
Scenes*

*The Memoir Workbook: A Step-by-Step Guide to Help You
Brainstorm, Organize, and Write Your Story*

CPSIA information can be obtained
at www.ICGtesting.com
Printed in the USA
FFHW010756050719
53425597-59106FF